Cambridge I

Elements in the Prc
edited b
Michael L. Peterson
Asbury Theological Seminary

GOD AND NON-HUMAN ANIMALS

Simon Kittle
Independent Scholar

CAMBRIDGE
UNIVERSITY PRESS

CAMBRIDGE
UNIVERSITY PRESS

Shaftesbury Road, Cambridge CB2 8EA, United Kingdom

One Liberty Plaza, 20th Floor, New York, NY 10006, USA

477 Williamstown Road, Port Melbourne, VIC 3207, Australia

314–321, 3rd Floor, Plot 3, Splendor Forum, Jasola District Centre,
New Delhi – 110025, India

103 Penang Road, #05–06/07, Visioncrest Commercial, Singapore 238467

Cambridge University Press is part of Cambridge University Press & Assessment,
a department of the University of Cambridge.

We share the University's mission to contribute to society through the pursuit of
education, learning and research at the highest international levels of excellence.

www.cambridge.org
Information on this title: www.cambridge.org/9781009598392

DOI: 10.1017/9781009296205

First published 2025

A catalogue record for this publication is available from the British Library

ISBN 978-1-009-59839-2 Hardback
ISBN 978-1-009-29621-2 Paperback
ISSN 2754-8724 (online)
ISSN 2754-8716 (print)

God and Non-Human Animals

Elements in the Problems of God

DOI: 10.1017/9781009296205
First published online: February 2025

Simon Kittle
Independent Scholar
Author for correspondence: Simon Kittle, simon@simonkittle.com

Abstract: This Element explores the relevance of non-human animals to theology. It suggests that while Christian theology has so far been a thoroughly anthropocentric discipline, there are good reasons for treating animals as subjects worthy of theological reflection in their own right. The Element considers animals in the context of Christian ethics, investigates whether the violence and suffering found in evolutionary processes can be reconciled with a good God, and surveys some of the ways key theological doctrines may need to be altered in the light of what contemporary science teaches about human animals and non-humans.

Keywords: theology, animals, non-humans, evolution, morality

ISBNs: 9781009598392 (HB), 9781009296212 (PB), 9781009296205 (OC)
ISSNs: 2754-8724 (online), 2754-8716 (print)

Contents

1 Animals and Theology   1

2 Non-Sapiens and Christian Ethics   10

3 Evolutionary Violence and the Character of God   22

4 Non-Sapiens, the Image of God, Redemption   44

References   65

1 Animals and Theology

Christian theology has been, and largely still is, a thoroughly anthropocentric discipline: not only do its primary concerns revolve around modern human beings, the discipline almost universally endorses the idea that modern humans, *Homo sapiens*, are unique among animals in a way that means the interests of sapiens ought always – or at least, almost always – have priority over the interests of other creatures.[1] Relative to standard theological fare, there is little discussion of animals in the history of Christian thought. What discussions there are tend, as Ryan McLaughlin has highlighted, to concern 'animals as revelatory to humans; animals as subjects of communion with humans; [or] animals as resources to be used by humans' – which is to say, animals are discussed only inasmuch as they impinge on human concerns (McLaughlin 2023). The twin ideas that animals might be subjects worthy of theological reflection in their own right and that they might deserve serious ethical consideration did not feature prominently in the Christian tradition until the second half of the twentieth century. Prior to this, the dominant view was that animals had little-to-no intrinsic worth and could be treated in any way that furthers the ends of humans. Thomas Aquinas is representative here:

> Now all animals are naturally subject to man. This can be proved in three ways. First, from the order observed by nature; ... as the plants make use of the earth for their nourishment, and animals make use of plants, man makes use of both plants and animals. It is in keeping with the order of nature, that man should be master over animals. Secondly, ... as man, being made to the image of God, is above other animals, these are rightly subject to his government. Thirdly, we see in [other animals] a certain participated prudence of natural instinct ... whereas man possesses a universal prudence ... [t]herefore the subjection of other animals to man is proved. (Aquinas 1947, I, Q. 96, A. 1)

Aquinas was clear about what followed from this:

> The love of charity extends to none but God and our neighbor. But the word neighbor cannot be extended to irrational creatures, since they have no fellowship with man in the rational life. Therefore charity does not extend to irrational creatures. (Aquinas 1947, II-II, Q. 25, A. 3)

---

[1] Whether theology would have prioritised the interests of *Homo sapiens* over the interests of other human species, such as *Homo erectus*, had such species overlapped with theology's beginning, is a fascinating question we have been saved from asking because (in all likelihood) our ancestors drove to extinction those species they were coextensive with. Theological reflection on the fact that we are, in Yuval Harari's (2015, p. 74) words, "the deadliest species in the annals of biology" lies beyond the scope of this work.

> If a man's affection [i.e., the psychological attitude which moves one to action] be one of reason, it matters not how man behaves to animals, because God has subjected all things to man's power, according to Ps. 8:8 ... and it is in this sense that the Apostle says that 'God has no care for oxen'; ... God does not ask of man what he does with oxen. (Aquinas 1947, I–II, Q. 102, A. 6, ad. 8)

Aquinas does say that if one is moved to action by pity for a suffering animal, one should refrain from certain forms of cruelty towards them. But lest we think that Aquinas considered this cruelty wrong because of the distress it causes the animals, he corrects us: 'if a man practice a pitiful affection for animals, he is all the more disposed to take pity on his fellow-men', and for this reason, to 'inculcate pity' in the ancient Israelites, God 'forbade them to do certain things savoring of cruelty to animals' (Aquinas 1947, I–II, Q. 102, A. 6, ad. 8). The merely instrumental reason for avoiding cruelty to animals expressed here is morally problematic. Some of Aquinas' contemporary apologists have pointed out that elsewhere Aquinas makes remarks that can be read as suggestive of a more positive attitude towards non-humans. The enormous effort expended on excavating this thread of thought is unsurprising given Aquinas' semi-canonical status, but identifying a handful of comments in a 2-million-word corpus that, if interpreted 'correctly', support a more robust eschewal of cruelty does little to blunt the basic point, which is that a straightforward reading of Aquinas minimises concern for animals, and such a reading has had an immense influence on the Christian tradition.[2] Hence we find relatively recent writers in the Thomist tradition making such claims as:

> We have no duties to [brute beasts] – not of justice ... ; not of religion ... ; not of fidelity ... ; We have ... no duties of charity, nor duties of any kind, to the lower animals. (Rickaby 1901, pp. 248–249)

> Since animals have no rights they cannot suffer injury in the strict sense of the word. (Prummer 1957, p. 109)

> Since animals cannot experience 'good' in a rational way, it is only in a limited way that we can love them. Since animals have no free choice, this is the basic factor of distinction. ... Animals show affection and loyalty, but in a trained or programmed sense. ... Fundamentally, animals cannot be a part of the human community; ... animals are not capable of sharing in [eternal beatitude], and thus we cannot properly extend Christian love to animals in this way. (Westberg 2015, p. 244)

---

[2] McLaughlin (2023, pp. 14–15) gives a helpful overview of the debate on whether Aquinas' theology can be read in an animal-friendly manner.

This negative attitude is not confined to the Catholic Thomist tradition nor to the Catholic tradition more widely. As Pieter Slootweg has shown, during the period 200–1600 C.E., the conviction of the 'triumvirate of Aristotle, Augustine and Aquinas' that 'animals should be excluded from proper moral consideration' was pivotal, with the result that animal suffering was 'considered morally irrelevant by all' (Slootweg 2021, pp. 30–32). Some Protestant thinkers, such as John Calvin, denied that non-human animals experienced any feelings at all (Slootweg 2021, 29 fn. 161). That non-human animals were denied reason and excluded from moral concern meant there was little impetus for thinkers to develop theological treatments of animals. And this only began to change in the eighteenth century (Slootweg 2021, pp. 116ff). Given this inheritance and its enduring influence – even today theological students typically cut their teeth on the likes of Augustine, Aquinas, and Calvin – it is no surprise to find, for instance, the renowned Lutheran theologian Robert Jenson suggesting in 1999 that the animal rights movement is founded on an 'anthropological nihilism' which leads ultimately to Nazism (Jenson 1999, pp. 56–57).

It is true that, if we mine deeply enough, we can find discussions of animals by Christians that appear to be more positive in character. Writings on the lives of the saints contain celebrations of compassion towards non-humans and sometimes depict saints as interacting positively with animals. Similarly, the richly illustrated medieval bestiaries present detailed descriptions of non-humans and their behaviour which, in some cases, reveal accurate attention to the lives of non-humans. There is also the strange phenomenon of putting animals on trial which, it might be argued, reveals a substantial view of the capacities of animals (more on this in Section 4.6). These minority reports show that it is too simple to say that the Christian tradition exhibits either an exclusively negative attitude or a wholesale disregard of non-human animals.

Yet, while this diversity in the tradition should not be overlooked, nor should we overdo any claim that its existence mitigates the thrust of the dominant theological position, a position which excludes from view the concerns of non-human animals. Indeed, on closer inspection, there is ambiguity in these minority reports. Ingvild Gilhus, drawing from the work of Steve Baker, notes that just as the animals depicted in fairy tales and children's cartoons are 'not animals in any meaningful way, only a medium for messages that concern humans', so something similar might be 'at work in Christian antiquity' (Gilhus 2006, pp. 6–7). When hyenas, geese, and frogs are portrayed as agreeing, promising, and obeying, in response to the spoken commands of saints (Waddell and Gibbings 1995), they are being imbued with a linguistic comprehension they do not possess, and so not being accurately represented as the animals they are. Similar misrepresentation occurs when non-humans are put forward as exemplars of particular moral traits. Works which portray animals or animal behaviour as virtuous or vicious and, on such grounds, attempt to draw moral lessons for humans only confirm the anthropocentrism of the tradition, even if they simultaneously witness to a minority view that lauded showing compassion towards animals.

Alongside this ambiguity in the minority reports is a more straightforward point, namely, that it is the dominant theological tradition, as opposed to the minority (primarily literary) traditions, that has wielded and continues to wield vast influence on the belief and practice of Christians everywhere. Millions of believers spanning numerous traditions have spent hours immersing themselves in Augustine, Aquinas, and Calvin, but Ælfric's *Lives of the Saints*? Less so. Key theological ideas of the dominant tradition – that humans are made in the image of God, that creation is ordered around humans, and that the universe is ever progressing towards the final redemption of humans – permeate Western thought and culture, even in its secular forms. The pervasive influence of theology as compared with hagiography or bestiary is perhaps why C. S. Lewis did not encounter much objection when he wrote in 1940 that '[b]easts are to be understood only in their relation to man and through man to God' (Lewis 1940, p. 142), and why few of his contemporary readers bat any eyelids upon encountering this statement.

A very good case can be made, then, for affirming that the vast majority of Christian theology is speciesist in the following sense: the interests of human beings are given undue weight over the interests of creatures belonging to other species (Berkman 2014, p. 14). As John Berkman has argued, however, it may be too kind to call theology speciesist. The label 'speciesist' suggests that Christian theologians have paid attention to non-human animals and argued that human interests should take precedence over those of non-human animals. The reality, argues Berkman, is closer to a 'moral nihilism' about other animals: most theologians have been indifferent to the interests and concerns of non-human animals (Berkman 2014, p. 16). I want to suggest that even the charge of moral nihilism may be too kind, since it fails to capture the negative implications of the dominant theological tradition. As A. Richard Kingston noted in 1967, with only 'a few noble exceptions theologians have done far more to discourage than to stimulate a concern for the lower creatures' (Kingston 1967, p. 482). The dominant theological understandings of what it is to be human produce a qualitative divide between sapiens and all other animals, a divide which implicitly denigrates the worth of other animals so that, whether or not Christian theology is essentially speciesist, it must be conceded that the Christian tradition has, in fact, helped to make possible the widespread maltreatment of animals. Kingston cites to this effect A. Jameson, who observed in

1854 that 'the primitive Christians by laying so much stress upon a future life, and placing the lower creatures out of the pale of hope, placed them at the same time out of the pale of sympathy, and thus laid the foundation for an utter disregard of animals' (Jameson, as cited in Kingston 1967, p. 482). This worry was famously articulated by Peter Singer, who argued in 1975 that the Christian claim that human life *and only human* life was sacred, 'served to confirm and further depress the lowly position nonhumans had in the Old Testament' (Singer 2002, p. 191), and while some have suggested that Singer's argument was too quick, one does not need much acquaintance with the history of Christian theology and practice to see there is some substance to the critique.

By the eighteenth century the belief that all animals had been created solely for human use had come to be widely rejected, but theological considerations of non-human animals in their own right remained sparse until the second half of the twentieth century. In 1956, C. W. Hume published *The Status of Animals in the Christian Religion*, where he noted that '[d]uring the past thousand years consideration for animals has, on the whole, lain outside the purview of Christian theology', but '[i]n quite recent times ... several Christian communions have taken official cognizance of animals' rights' (Hume 1956, p. 1). After Brigid Brophy instigated the modern animal rights movement with her 1965 article 'The Rights of Animals',[3] theological engagement with non-humans picked up, due in no small part due to the work of Andrew Linzey (1976, 1987, 1994, 1998, 2009a). Other important works include Jay McDaniel's *Of God and Pelicans* (1989), Stephen Webb's *On God and Dogs* (1998), David Clough's *On Animals* (2012; 2019), Ryan McLaughlin's *Christian Theology and the Status of Animals* (2014), Eric Meyers' *Inner Animalities* (2018), and Clair Linzey's *Developing Animal Theology* (2022).[4] These and other thinkers have explored what it would mean to treat animals as subjects worthy of theological reflection. Unfortunately, this work, largely 'neglected by the theological world' (Linzey 1994, p. vii), has had 'little effect on the actions of religious leaders' (Farains 2011, p. 102), and little effect on religious believers in general – an illustration of the point made above about the immense influence on the Christian mind of figures like Augustine and Aquinas. Two thousand years of anthropocentric theological sediment is not easily overcome.

The speciesist and nihilistic stances towards animals exhibited by most theology are problematic for several reasons. First, animals are the subject of a life, and many have needs, desires, and are sentient, possessing an interest

---

[3] See Richard Ryder (1989, pp. 5–7) for details of Brophy's influence.

[4] There has also been much recent interest in the philosophical problems posed to theism by animal pain and suffering. See Murray (2008), Creegan (2013), and Dougherty (2014).

in what happens to them. Second, animals are a significant part of God's creation, which gives prima facie reason to think they are valuable to God in a way that demands attention. Third, the dominant stance cannot justify, but only reinforces, the current ethical practice of Christians – this is a problem because current ethical practice exhibits several inconsistencies. Fourth, given what we know about the way the life on earth evolved, knowledge of other animals contributes to our understanding of our own humanity. This is true not just because we human beings are biologically continuous with other animals but also because, as Eric Meyer (2018) has stressed, human concepts are formed using difference, so our understanding of what it is to be human depends in part on how we conceive of non-humans.[5]

These issues are difficult to treat in a judicious manner because, as Mary Midgley put it, 'a sense of unreality often blocks our attempts to understand our moral relations with animals' (1983, p. 9). James Rachels explains:

> [E]ven as we try to think objectively about what animals are like, we are burdened with the need to justify our moral relations with them. We kill animals for food; we use them as experimental subjects in laboratories; we exploit them as sources of raw materials such as leather and wool; . . . Thus, when we think about what the animals are like, we are motivated to conceive of them in ways that are compatible with treating them in these ways. (Rachels 1990, p. 129)

Indeed, motivated reasoning is rife both in our thinking about other animals and in theology, and is hard to challenge. Making significant progress may require the development of what Berkman (2014) calls *theological ethology*, a theological subdiscipline focused on animals that would feed into and form part of a systematic theology. In this work, I aim to adopt something close to the method of Andrew Linzey's *animal theology*, as succinctly described by Clair Linzey:

> Animal theology is an attempt to view the Christian tradition through an animal-friendly lens, while retaining a critical approach to the tradition with regard to its concern for animals. Animal theology is involved, like feminist theology, in a process of looking again at the Christian tradition to reclaim and rebuild insights and voices concerning our relationship with animals. (Linzey 2022, p. 3)

A note on language is required. The words and concepts we use, the way we describe things, and our habits of language affect *what* we think about and, to some degree, *what it is possible* for us to think about. Moreover, our words and

---

[5] For more on the relevance of non-human animals to Christian doctrine, see Clough (2012, pp. xii–xiv).

concepts are rarely neutral. They evoke what cognitive linguist George Lakoff calls a *frame*: a set of associations, beliefs, and sometimes behaviours that attach to a term and which typically embed myriad value judgements. Lakoff gives the following example:

> On the day that George W. Bush arrived in the White House, the phrase *tax relief* started coming out of the White House. It was repeated almost every day thereafter, was used by the press . . ., and became so much a part of public discourse that liberals started using it. Think of the framing for relief. For there to be relief, there must be an affliction, an afflicted party, and a reliever who removes the affliction. . . . When the word tax is added to relief, the result is a metaphor: Taxation is an affliction. And the person who takes it away is a hero, and anyone who tries to stop him is a bad guy. (Lakoff 2014, pp. 1–2)

This is an example of a politically skewed frame because it plays into the interests of those who desire and stand to benefit from low taxation, or the minimalist state with which it is often associated. If taxation was referred to as *dues*, *societal contributions*, or *cooperation costs*, a very different frame would be evoked, and with it an alternative set of value judgements.

When it comes to non-humans, we human animals have for millennia used language to both distance ourselves from and lower the status of other animals. The terms we use for animals routinely become insults when applied to humans. This is true for general terms, such as the noun 'beast' (which has the secondary meaning of 'an annoying or cruel human person') and the adjective 'beastly' (which means 'unkind or unpleasant'),[6] and for more specific terms, such as 'chicken' (as in, to chicken out), 'fishy' (to be a cause of suspicion), 'rat' (as in, to be a 'dirty rat' or to 'rat on' someone), and 'hog' (as in, to take more of one's share of something).

This might seem straightforward, even trivial, but it barely scratches the surface of the importance of language. Carol Adams (2010) has argued that the way human language occludes our abuse of animals is pervasive and systematic. Adams applies Margaret Homans' notion of the *absent referent* to the topic of non-human animals. One of Adams' fundamental insights is that our use of language serves to disguise the nature of our interactions with other animals such that the living, breathing animal which becomes food for us and, in particular, the *death* of that living, breathing animal, become *absent referents* during the act of eating (Adams 2010, p. 13). Put otherwise, our habits of language make it extremely difficult for us to refer to the killing and death of the animals we consume. This makes it hard to think clearly about them:

---

[6] As Keith Thomas reminds us, it is "no accident that the symbol of Anti-Christ was the Beast" (1983, p. 36).

The 'absent referent' is that which separates the meat eater from the animal and the animal from the end product. The function of the absent referent is to keep our 'meat' separated from any idea that she or he was once an animal, to keep the 'moo' or 'cluck' or 'baa' away from the meat, to keep something from being seen as having been someone. (Adams 2010, p. 13)

Adams' analysis is sophisticated and powerful. It explains the disconnect between the living, breathing, experiencing animal and the meat it becomes, and it highlights why and how the image of meat can come to be used to refer to women, or aspects of women's experience, in a manner that confirms 'the connection between the oppression of women and the oppression of animals' (Adams 2010, p. 13). Unfortunately, I cannot do justice here to Adams' analysis; however, I can at least describe some of the ways '[a]nimals are made absent through language that renames dead bodies before consumers participate in eating them' (Adams 2010, p. 66).

To begin with, then, we do not refer to the bodies of the animals we kill for food as dead bodies or corpses – if they referred to at all, they are called *carcasses* or *produce*. We do not talk about eating animal flesh or animal muscle but of eating meat, which 'our culture further mystifies ... with gastronomic language, so we do not conjure dead, butchered animals, but cuisine': the dead pig becomes bacon or pork; the dead cow becomes steak (Adams 2010, p. 66). And of course, once we've killed baby animals, we never refer to them as baby animals but as veal or lamb (Adams 2010, p. 66). The species that humans have bred to be more submissive, to gain weight quicker, to produce more eggs, and so on are referred to as *farm animals*, a label on a par with *sea creatures* in suggesting that *being on a farm* is the position ordained for such animals in God's cosmic hierarchy. The living, breathing animals are also lost from view in the numerous euphemisms that are used to hide what we do, or cause to be done, to the animals we consume. Henry Mance reports that some in agriculture describe the sending of animals on their hours-long journey to slaughter as the animals 'going off farm' (Mance 2021, p. 48), as if the animals are just popping out for a bit. Others refer to the slaughter of 'spent', four-year-old dairy cows – in reality, not spent, but utterly exhausted and stressed due to repeated forced impregnation, having their calves taken from them, and being fed large doses of antibiotics and growth hormone to maximise their 'efficiency' – as 'reforming' the cows (Ricard 2016, Ch 4 fn. 6). When manta ray, hammerhead sharks, puffer fish, green turtles, and sea horses – to mention just 5 of the 145 species that could have been cited – are caught up in the mile-long trawler nets designed to catch bluefin tuna, they are often referred to simply as 'bycatch', a term that Jonathan Safran Foer suggests is the quintessential example of the metaphorical use of the word 'bullshit'

(Foer 2009, p. 49). Such examples of misdirection in language could be multiplied,[7] and are made possible by a culture which is adept at 'cannibalizing the experience of animals' through the use of animal-involving metaphors to describe our own experience, as when we describe someone as a scapegoat, or a guinea pig, or say that someone is flogging a dead horse (Adams 2010, p. 94).[8] Such examples begin to shed light on how animals *are* thought about (e.g., as produce) and *are not* thought about (e.g., as sentient beings).

These unhelpful patterns of language use are often found in contemporary theological works. For instance, despite recognising that the term 'beast' is problematic, Eleonore Stump uses the term in her recent book *The Image of God*, defending this on the grounds that 'in some circles [the term "beast"] retains the affectionate connotations it has in the widely known Christmas carol about the friendly beasts' (Stump 2022, 312 fn. 8). Since referring to other animals as beasts reinforces the association between non-human animals and undesirable qualities while simultaneously implying those negative qualities are not shared by humans, Stump's justification of the use of the term might be considered an example of how relatively trivial human interests – for example, the love of a Christmas carol – are routinely placed above the interests of non-human animals – for example, their interest in not being referred to in a way that makes their abuse easier.[9]

Addressing this problem is no easy task. The label 'non-human animal' is clunky and still suggests a hard-and-fast demarcation between humans and all other animals. The same is true of 'other than human animals'.[10] As Jacques Derrida noted, such demarcations also 'corral a large number of living beings within a single concept' in a way that is unhelpful because it makes it harder to attend to the particularities of the individual in front of us (Derrida 2002, p. 400). I cannot avoid these distinctions entirely, since this work engages with conceptual systems that centre on them. I attempt to mitigate the problem by varying the terminology I employ, and by sometimes employing the term 'sapiens' to refer to modern *Homo sapiens*, which also helps us remember that there have existed other human species whose existence is not irrelevant to theology.

---

[7] See Adams (2010, Ch 3).

[8] It is worth remembering this metaphor's literal origin: just 200 years ago horses were routinely flogged to death on English streets during attempts to have them carry impatient stagecoach passengers that little bit further; the first animal welfare legislation ever proposed aimed to stop this practice – it didn't pass Mance (2021, p. 28).

[9] Just as a human infant has an interest in not being harmed, despite being unable to understand the idea of an interest, so too non-humans can have interests, even if they cannot understand the concept.

[10] Meyer (2018, p. 174) provides an excellent discussion of the conceptual difficulties that give rise to this problem.

The plan for this work is as follows. In Section 2, I argue that inconsistencies in the ethical belief and practice dominant in the West[11] give rise to the following dilemma: either it is the case that it is morally wrong to eat cats and dogs, but also pigs and cows, in which case, theists should refrain from eating pigs and cows, or, it is not morally wrong to eat pigs or cows, but neither is it wrong to eat cats or dogs. I show that three prominent theological rationalisations for eating animals provide no way to address this dilemma.

In Section 3, I consider various strategies for reconciling the evils of evolutionary violence with theism. Responses can be classified according to whether or not they endorse a cosmic fall, and after assessing responses on both sides of this division, I conclude that the idea of a personal God may be reconcilable with evolutionary violence only if we significantly revise our concept of God.

In Section 4, I aim to show that attending seriously to non-human animals will have significant implications for several key areas of theology. I outline some of the ways our knowledge of other animals has already required departures from the theology dominant throughout most of Christian history. I then look at some of the ways scholars have begun the positive task of rethinking the image of God and the Incarnation in light of non-humans.

2 Non-Sapiens and Christian Ethics

Whatever else be true, whether there be gods or only atoms, whether men are significantly superior to non-human animals or no, whether there be a life to come or this poor accident be all, this at least cannot be true, that it is proper to be the cause of avoidable ill. . . . And if this minimal principle be accepted, there is no other honest course than the immediate rejection of all flesh-foods and most biomedical research.

Stephen R. L. Clark, *The Moral Status of Animals*, Preface.

2.1 Introduction

Christian ethicists have largely ignored non-human animals. The *New Studies in Christian Ethics* series of monographs published by Cambridge University Press contains, as of late 2024, thirty-eight volumes dedicated to topics as specific as healthcare funding or market complicity, but has no volume which treats of non-sapiens in a systematic way. Key textbooks on Christian ethics, including those widely used on university curricula, frequently fail to include any sustained discussion of non-human animals, save perhaps for a brief

---

[11] It is a limitation of this work that it is written by, and primarily addressed to, someone living in the West.

mention in sections on the environment.[12] The same is true of companion and handbook volumes.[13]

Part of the reason for this is undoubtedly the thoroughly anthropocentric character of Christian theology, including twenty-first-century theology. Another part of the explanation may be the operation of psychological defence mechanisms. The ethical practice of most Christians in developed nations is, just like the ethical practice of most non-Christians in developed nations, deeply inconsistent when it comes to the treatment of animals. The inconsistency is deep in that how we treat other animals is at odds with how we like to see ourselves, namely, as people who are trying our best to be morally good. But the inconsistency is deep in another, far more potent way, too: when a person who consumes animal flesh, animal skin, or the reproductive fruits of female animals is confronted with the realities of how these animals – our evolutionary cousins – are treated in making those 'products', it is common to intuit right away that acting on that information would require one to change beliefs and habits that are frequently part of one's identity. This is especially so for men because, as Carol Adams has shown, the act of eating dead animals is thought in Western cultures to be a key element of masculinity. This can lead us to engage in motivated reasoning when it comes to thinking about pigs, cows, chickens, sheep, and the other animals we consume. This motivated reasoning, rarely fully explicit or clearly articulated, may proceed something like the following:

> The treatment of animals described by animal rights activists is truly horrible, and morally abhorrent; if that treatment really occurred, it would be morally wrong to consume animals; but I consume animals, and I'm a decent enough person. Plus, I could never become a vegetarian or vegan, because . . . . I love bacon sandwiches too much! [. . . or, I hate vegetables . . . or, vegetarianism is a feminine thing, or, veganism is a liberal fad, and so on]. And since I'm not going to stop eating bacon, and I'm basically a good person, that information about how animals are treated must be wrong: animals don't suffer like that on most farms, or maybe they don't suffer at all since they don't have souls, or . . .

To be clear, the suggestion is not that we consciously and deliberately engage in such reasoning. Rather, this sort of reasoning is typically implicit, something that occurs 'in a flash' without any extended conscious thought process. It is more *felt* than *discursively thought*. Such reasoning operates to defend our

---

[12] See, e.g., Banner (1999), Cunningham (2008), Mathewes (2010), Wogaman (2011), Nullens and Michener (2013), Wells et al. (2017) – at the time of writing all of these works were found on undergraduate reading lists in theological ethics at top universities.

[13] See, e.g., Hauerwas and Wells (2011), Gill (2012), and Long and Miles (2023), none of which have a chapter on animals.

conception of who we are and what we do. Often the result of such reasoning is, to employ words from Ursula K. Le Guin, that 'most devoted ally' of oppressive practices, 'the averted eye' (Le Guin 2002, p. 335). It enables us ignore the suffering experienced by the pig we are eating, and get on with our lives. Such motivated thinking is routine in everyday life. For instance, in one study psychologists found that '[i]f you give someone a beef snack and ask them whether cows suffer pain, they are less likely to say yes than if you give them some nuts' (Mance 2021, p. 63). It is difficult to overcome such reasoning precisely because, being implicit and habitual, it is not easily accessible to conscious reflection and, serving to defend our conception of who we are, we prefer not to submit it to conscious reflection anyway.

In light of this, instead of assessing the reasons Christians have for thinking that eating animals is morally wrong, I approach the topic a little more indirectly. In 2.2, I recount empirical findings which suggest that pigs and cows are as intellectually capable and emotionally complex as cats and dogs.[14] This strongly suggests they should be given roughly equal moral consideration. We are thus faced with a dilemma: either conclude that it is morally wrong to eat pigs and cows, or conclude that it is morally permissible to eat cats and dogs. In 2.3 I show that three explicitly theological defences of eating animals provide no way out of this dilemma.

2.2 The Rock of Inconsistency

The inconsistency in contemporary ethical practice is straightforward to illustrate: picture the cat or dog with which you are most familiar – your cat or dog, your family's, your neighbour's – and then ask yourself whether you would eat that cat or dog. I do not mean, ask yourself whether you can imagine some ludicrous set of circumstances – stuck on a desert island; facing down a zombie apocalypse – where you would, maybe, just maybe, judge it permissible to eat the cat or dog. I mean, ask yourself whether it would be morally unproblematic[15] to get home after a normal day at school or work, not subject to any significant stressors, plenty of other food in the fridge, and eat the cat or dog in question. I've not met anyone who answers 'yes'. Many people refuse to answer, finding the suggestion too horrific to contemplate. Fair enough. But what does this attitude reveal? That the vast majority of people in the West find the prospect of eating a dog horrific is not, I take it, evidence of a widespread

---

[14] I focus here on how we should treat pigs and cows, but key theological ideas (e.g., that humans have dominion over non-humans) may well give rise to obligations to wild animals. See Crummett (2022).

[15] If you think the illegality of buying and selling cat or dog meat is influencing your moral judgements, imagine you live in a jurisdiction where such commerce is legal.

over-sentimentality towards canines. Rather, it reveals that, being well acquainted with dogs, we intuit right away that they are individuals who can feel joy and pain, that they enjoy certain things and dislike others, that they feel scared at times, excited at others. And, being aware of this, we implicitly form the judgement that it would be morally wrong to kill and eat a dog.

But now consider the fact that multiple lines of evidence have shown that pigs 'are in no way less conscious, less sensitive to pain, or less intelligent than our cats and dogs' (Ricard 2016, p. 4). Pigs experience episodic memory (Pouca et al. 2021, p. 149); they have a neural biology underlying the experience of emotions that is similar to that found in us sapiens, and are known to experience emotions that can lead to long-term depression (Torgerson-White 2022, p. 273); they are known to experience negative emotions of high arousal (i.e., fear) and of low arousal (i.e., sadness), demonstrating different behavioural responses in each case – responses akin to those we find in humans (Torgerson-White 2022, p. 274). Pigs are able to move their tails and ears, 'and the way they do so is influenced by the way they are feeling' (Torgerson-White 2022, p. 275). Pigs form stable social groups and cooperate to build communal nests (Singer 2002, p. 120). They may be able to recognise 'as many as thirty different individual pigs in their group', greeting those to whom they are closest (Joy 2011, p. 42). Their social groups have dominance hierarchies, and the pigs are aware of these hierarchies and 'use that [knowledge] to their own advantage', something which suggests that 'pigs are capable of a theory of mind, acting on the knowledge of others' (Murdock 2022, p. 447). Pigs engage in play, become unsettled when they observe other pigs suffering, and are adept at problem solving. Piglets as young as three weeks can learn to respond to their names (Joy 2011, p. 42). Matthieu Ricard recounts how:

> Stanley Curtis of the University of Pennsylvania taught pigs to play a video game utilizing a joystick modified so they could manipulate it with their snout. Not only did they really learn to play, but they did so significantly faster than a trained dog and as fast as a chimpanzee, thus demonstrating an amazing capacity for abstract representation. (Ricard 2016, p. 121)

Kenneth Kephart showed that pigs were equally as good as dogs at 'lifting a latch in order to get out of their pen', and that they often 'go so far as to open the pens of other pigs to let them out' (Ricard 2016, p. 121). This helping behaviour may be because pigs have some ability to adopt the perspective of other pigs (Murdock 2022, p. 448). The high level of emotional sensitivity and intelligence possessed by pigs means that '[like] humans who have endured solitary confinement and other tortures in captivity, pigs [reared in factory farms] have engaged in self-mutilation, and have been found repeating the same nonsensical behaviors over and over' (Joy 2011, p. 43).

Like pigs, cattle are a 'highly social animal' (Marino 2022, p. 859). They live in herds for protection against predators and form strong bonds with other members of the herd. The bond between cow and calf is especially strong. Calves as young as three weeks can recognise and respond to their mother's call, in contradistinction to the calls of others in the herd (Marino 2022, p. 861); as they mature, the calf also forms 'lasting bonds' with other members of the herd (Marino 2022, p. 858). Cows would naturally suckle their calves for between six and twelve months (Joy 2011, p. 51). Henry Mance reports that in industrialised dairy production calves are 'standardly taken from their mothers' between twenty-four and forty-eight hours after being born (Mance 2021, p. 69). This separation causes distress due to the intimacy of the bond between cow and calf (Joy 2011, p. 61). Boris Cyrulnik explains that by separating a calf from its mother, 'you provoke extremely intense suffering, true despair. ... Both cow and calf have been deprived of what made sense for them' (Cyrulnik, as cited in Ricard 2016, p. 106). After separation cows will bellow for days. And the distress caused to the calf can be long-lasting: studies have shown that two-year-old cows who were separated from their mothers are less active and less exploratory than peers who were not separated (Mance 2021, p. 67). This treatment of cows and calves differs markedly, of course, with how we treat kittens and puppies, who are usually kept with their mothers for at least eight weeks after being born.

Both calves and adult bovines can distinguish different humans based on prior experience, even when those people are wearing the same uniform (Marino 2022, p. 859). One study has shown that cows can recognise members of their own social group from 2D photographs (Coulon et al. 2009). Research has shown that 'cows [use] vocalizations to express emotions in positive and negative contexts and that individuals recognized known conspecifics' vocalizations' (Murdock 2022, p. 448), and that '[t]here is evidence for specific meaning in cow vocalizations' (Marino 2022, p. 861). Cows also have a very good spatial memory, something that is important for grazing animals. In a Hebb-Williams closed-field test, which measures how well creatures are able to navigate a maze when detours are required, cows 'performed favorably compared with ... dogs' (Marino 2022, p. 860). It is no surprise to learn, then, that fear is communicated among individuals in a herd (Torgerson-White 2022, p. 274), or that cows at slaughter show the marks of increased negative emotions: increased heart rate and elevated cortisol and adrenaline (Torgerson-White 2022, p. 274).

All of this suggests that the subjective experience of pigs and cows is as varied, complex, and nuanced as the subjective experience of cats and dogs. And this implies that pigs and cows deserve at least as much moral consideration as cats and dogs. This does not mean we need to treat these creatures in identical ways: what is good for the cat isn't necessarily good for the dog, or cow. But it does undermine the idea that there might be a morally salient reason why it would be permissible to kill and eat pigs and cows but not permissible to kill and eat cats and dogs. We therefore face a dilemma: if we agree it is morally wrong to eat a cat or a dog, we should also think it wrong to eat a pig or a cow; alternatively, if we insist it is permissible to eat pigs and cows, we should conclude it is also permissible to eat cats and dogs. Consistency demands one of these responses.[16]

As already mentioned, I think we are correct when we judge it morally wrong to eat cats and dogs. This is not a 'thin' moral judgement. It is a 'thick' moral judgement that derives from extended acquaintance with, and attention to, cats and dogs. It is because the bonds between us sapiens and the cats and dogs we live with are so deep that most people find the idea of eating a cat or a dog morally repugnant. The depth of these bonds reveals to us that cats and dogs are individuals, with unique dispositions and characters, as well as needs and interests they want to satisfy. We would come to think the same way of pigs and cows, were it possible for us to see them as individuals. In their book *Theology on the Menu*, David Grumett and Rachel Muers note that it is increasingly recognised that some forms of ethical judgement can and should be taken seriously as sources of theological understanding (Grumett and Muers 2010, p. 142). This is what I claim for the judgement that it is wrong to eat cats and dogs: it is the correct ethical response to an encounter with these sentient others. Since this is, or would be, true for pigs and cows too, I conclude it is morally wrong to eat pigs and cows, just as it is wrong to eat cats and dogs.

Significantly, the argument above does not rely on the claim that dogs, cats, pigs, and cows possess rights. Nor does it require endorsing any particular metaethical theory (other than the rejection of error theory about ethical judgements). There are accounts of Christian ethics which ground (some of) ethics in, for instance, hospitality (Hobgood-Oster 2010, Ch 4), or neighbourly love (Miller 2010, Ch 6), or theos-rights (Linzey 1987), and which conclude (or come close to concluding) that eating animals is morally problematic. These works are valuable explorations of the foundations of religious ethics. But the argument I've presented relies on no such machinery, and so cannot be

---

[16] The dilemma as stated concerns only pigs and cows, but I think it could be extended to cover several other taxa of creature that are routinely used for their flesh, skin, or eggs.

refuted by pointing to the inadequacies of such theories. Neither does it rely on establishing that raising and slaughtering non-human animals for food causes them to suffer.[17]

Before considering whether theological defences of eating animals may dissolve this dilemma, I wish to highlight two points.

First, it might be objected that the argument above relies on the claim – implausible, because too narrow – that it is cognitive and emotional capacities alone which bestow moral standing. But nothing in the argument relies on this, or the closely related view that 'whatever is sentient, but only what is sentient, has moral standing' (Wennberg 2003, p. 38). The argument is consistent with the claim that non-sentient life and ecosystems have intrinsic moral value. It requires only that, whatever considerations lead us to conclude it is wrong to kill and eat cats and dogs parallel considerations also apply when it comes to pigs and cows.

Second, I believe that the argument presented here is consistent with the feminist care tradition in ethics. Writers in that tradition have been critical of arguments that appeal to abstract, universally possessed properties in order to generate (near-)universal obligations. Such arguments tend to downplay differences among individuals and their social and relational contexts and this, as Lori Gruen highlights, tends to result in a style of theorising that favours men (Gruen 2007, p. 333). Yet the validity of that critique does not preclude the existence of universal obligations. Indeed, pioneering theorists in feminist care ethics such as Carol Adams and Josephine Donovan have been at the forefront of making a feminist case for the impermissibility of eating animals. As Donovan and Adams see it, an ethic-of-care approach leads to the view that:

> It is wrong to harm sentient creatures unless overriding good will result for them. It is wrong to kill such animals unless in immediate self-defense or in defense of those for whom one is personally responsible. (Donovan and Adams 2007, p. 4)

They go on to say that attempts to view animals as communicating others while also seeing them as food 'is obviously incompatible with a care ethic which requires that humans heed what the "communicative others" are telling them – invariably that they do not want to be killed and eaten' (Donovan and Adams 2007, p. 13). Thus, while the argument I have presented does lead to the view that those living in the West who judge it wrong to eat cats and dogs should also judge it wrong to eat pigs and cows, I think this is consistent with grounding morality in care for the other. It is also consistent with the valuable feminist

---

[17] Foer (2009) and Ricard (2016) both present a detailed case for this claim.

insight that a full ethical regard for others requires not just refraining from causing them harm but doing what we can to dismantle the unjust structures that facilitate such harm in the first place (Donovan and Adams 2007, p. 14).

2.3 Theological Defences of the Moral Permissibility of Eating Animals

In this section I assess three theological justifications for eating animals presented by prominent theologians. I conclude that they provide no way of avoiding the dilemma presented in the previous subsection.

2.3.1 Southgate

Christopher Southgate discusses two approaches people have used to argue for a theological vegetarianism: the *protological approach* and the *eschatological approach* (Southgate 2008a, p. 247). The protological approach suggests that Christians should adopt a vegetarian diet because 'God originally intended that the created order should be ... a vegetarian world' (Southgate 2008a, p. 247). This is inferred from the first creation narrative in Genesis, the key verses being Genesis 1:29–30, where God gives all living creatures – including us sapiens – every plant and seed-bearing tree for food. Those who appeal to this text often point out that sapiens were given dominion over other animals *in the context of this original veganism* concluding, as Andrew Linzey memorably put it, that '[h]erb-eating dominion is hardly a license for tyranny' (Linzey 2001, p. 127). Broadening the point a little, Carol Adams writes:

> Whatever dominion humans have been granted over nonhuman animals is constrained not just by Genesis 1:29 and its dictates about food, but by the entire movement of God's creative acts up to this point. Humans and nonhuman animals are not the devourers of each other, but of plants. (Adams 2012, p. 6)

The eschatological approach to a theological vegetarianism makes the claim that God's ultimate goal for creation is for it to be peace-filled, without violence, pain, or suffering. This theological defence of vegetarianism or veganism can (but need not) be combined with the protological defence. The eschatological view is endorsed by Richard Young (2012), Linzey (1994), and others. The central texts used are Romans 8:19–21 – which states that creation is in bondage to decay and awaiting the liberty of the children of God – and Isaiah 11:6–9, 65:25 – the famous passage on God's peaceable kingdom where the wolf will lie down with the lamb. The basic thought is that, if the Kingdom of God is going to be a place without violence, pain, or suffering, then adopting a vegetarian diet now is, if not morally obligatory, at least the moral ideal, because it points towards God's ultimate plan for creation.

Southgate rejects both arguments because each is committed to the idea that there was a time in earth's history when living creatures existed but there was no violence (Southgate 2008a, p. 248). This can only be maintained if we posit a historical fall. This is straightforward for the protological argument, but also true of the eschatological argument. Defenders of the latter are committed to a historical fall because only thus can they claim that refraining from violence mirrors God's hopes for creation. If God created the violent processes in creation, then heaven may contain violence, and refraining from violence would not point towards God's ideal. Southgate thinks the idea of a historical fall is untenable because we learn from science that '[p]redation, violence, parasitism, suffering and extinction were integral parts of the natural order long before *Homo sapiens* ... [and are] more deeply embedded in the purposes of God than ... appeals to a historical Fall concede' (Southgate 2008a, pp. 249, 253).

Southgate's positive case for eating animals is based on the idea that it is *necessary* for the good of us human animals that we eat animals. Writing of the love that humans might have for other animals, he states:

> Such a love has to be a tough, discerning love, not mere sentiment but a real outworking of desire purified by kenosis. It is a love which recognizes that other creatures may have to be eaten ... for the human good – but still celebrates the wonder of their existence, and desires coexistence, indeed, desires that the other might know fullness of selving and flourishing as itself, and the fullest possible opportunity for self-transcendence. (Southgate 2008a, pp. 255–256)

Southgate contends here that non-human creatures *have to* be eaten for some goods of human existence to be realised – a point he makes explicit when he rejects Linzey's claim that 'conditions *now* make it possible, at least in developed countries, to subsist entirely without meat' (Southgate 2008a, p. 256 fn. 51). Although this claim is central to Southgate's argument, he doesn't explain *why* he thinks it is true. And we have very little reason to agree with it. A large and increasing number of sapiens can and do live entirely without consuming animals – and they don't just survive, but flourish. True, for a very small proportion of sapiens, medical conditions require the consumption of animal products if the person is to stay healthy. But this only shows that that small group of sapiens are morally permitted to consume animals – it does nothing to obviate the more general application of the dilemma.

Digging further into Southgate's position provides no additional resources for dissolving the dilemma, but only raises more problems. Southgate says, for instance, that we should treat other animals with great care, even entering into friendship with them (Southgate 2008b, p. 119). This will seem natural to anyone who has shared their home with a cat or a dog, but according to Southgate, such friendship is consistent with one of the friends – always the human animal in question, of course – killing and eating the other without their consent (Southgate 2008b, p. 121). It is unclear how to make sense of this, or how we might 'desire that the other might know fullness of selving' while also desiring that other's life be cut short so we can eat their flesh.

In any case, none of this provides any way to address the dilemma. If Southgate's defence of eating animals provided a moral justification for eating pigs and cows, it would also provide a moral justification for eating cats and dogs.

2.3.2 Bauckham

In his *Living with Other Creatures*, Richard Bauckham discusses some of the ethical issues raised by non-human animals. Bauckham's goal is to 'think out a properly Christian approach to' the ecological crises that we humans have caused by our abuse of non-human creation; he seeks an approach that draws from the central themes of Christian theology, acknowledges that 'God the Creator delights in and cares for all his creatures', and is thoroughly rooted in scripture (Bauckham 2011, p. xi). Bauckham's position is nicely captured in this passage:

> Jesus' attitude to animals belongs wholly within the Old Testament and Jewish tradition. In this tradition it was permitted to kill certain animals for sacrifice to God in the temple and for food. For Jesus to have rejected either of these practices in principle would have been a significant innovation. . . . [B]ut there is no evidence at all that he innovated in either of these two ways. (Bauckham 2011, p. 99)

For Bauckham, this settles the matter as far as any putative obligation Christians may have to be vegetarians: there is none. Bauckham leaves some of his reasoning implicit, but we can fill in the detail. Behind Bauckham's thinking are the twin ideas that Jesus is our moral exemplar and that Jesus is sinless. It follows from this pair of claims that emulating Jesus cannot be wrong. And therefore, if 'Jesus ate with his disciples the Passover lamb that had been sacrificed in the temple that afternoon', and if it can 'scarcely [be] doubt[ed] that [Jesus] ate meat other than that of sacrificial animals' (Bauckham 2011, pp. 100–101), we can conclude that it is morally permissible for Christians to eat non-human animals. Bauckham bolsters this conclusion by noting that Jesus did not disapprove of the livelihoods of those of his disciples who were fishermen; indeed, Jesus multiplied not just the loaves but the fishes, and 'not only cooked and served fish for the disciples … but also ate fish himself' (Bauckham 2011, p. 101).

According to Bauckham, we can therefore conclude that 'Jesus neither adopted vegetarianism for reasons that other Jews had for doing so nor adopted it for innovatory reasons of his own' (Bauckham 2011, p. 101). This does not rule out there being a 'valid Christian argument for vegetarianism' but, for Bauckham, it does mean that 'an argument that meat-eating is absolutely wrong would clearly contradict the Christian belief in the sinlessness of Jesus' (Bauckham 2011, p. 104).

The line of thinking Bauckham develops is harder to make work than it may first appear. Granted, Jesus is an exemplar for Christians. And granted, tradition holds that Jesus is sinless. It follows that nothing Jesus did was wrong. But that doesn't mean his followers can emulate *everything* Jesus did without sin. The tradition maintains, for instance, that Jesus claimed to be God. But it is not morally permissible for Jesus' followers to claim to be God. Moreover, it may be that it is permissible to eat animals only when that is required to live a healthy life. If first-century Palestine was such a context, no one living in that context would have done wrong by eating animals, but we would be unable to draw any general conclusion from that. The possibility of this shows that the moral permissibility of Jesus' eating animals does not transfer in any simple manner to our context today.

Once again, however, and as with Southgate's discussion, the main point here is that Bauckham's reasoning doesn't provide any way to escape the dilemma presented above. If Jesus' eating lamb and fish makes it permissible, as Bauckham seems to imply, for Christians to eat pork, then nothing in Bauckham's discussion of the ethics of eating animals is going to allow us to conclude that it is permissible to eat pigs and cows but wrong to eat cats and dogs.

2.3.3 Wirzba

Norman Wirzba's book *Food and Faith* (2011) discusses food 'in terms of its origin and end in God as the one who provides for, communes with, and ultimately reconciles creation' (Wirzba 2011, xii). Wirzba does not provide a systematic discussion of the ethics of consuming animals, but he does say why he rejects vegetarianism.

Central to Wirzba's theology of eating is the recognition that 'for any creature to live, countless seen and unseen others must die, often by being eaten themselves', that 'life as we know it *depends* on death' and '[d]eath is eating's steadfast accomplice' (Wirzba 2011, p. 1). Wirzba suggests that the best way to understand this theologically is through the lens of sacrifice, which is about 'God's self-offering way of being with the world' (Wirzba 2011, p. 133).

This theological understanding of sacrifice allows us reframe death as something that is, if not positive, then at least necessary, and something that is made sacred by God's own self-sacrifice. According to Wirzba, this means that Christians cannot fully accept God's gift of life without also accepting the death that was required to bring that life to fruition (Wirzba 2011, p. 133). The good we consume is 'a vast and unfathomably deep community of creatures that is sustained by God's sacrificial love' (Wirzba 2011, pp. 133–134).

To embrace vegetarianism or veganism for theological reasons is, therefore, to refuse 'to accept creation on God's terms, terms that bear witness to a sacrificial logic of life through death to new life' (Wirzba 2011, p. 135). None of this means, of course, that non-human animals can be treated in any manner we human animals find convenient. Wirzba thinks that modern factory farming is morally problematic (Wirzba 2011, pp. xiii, 131, 175):

> When people understand creation as the concrete manifestation of God's sacrificial love, then it is an imperative that food production and consumption recognize and honor the costly grace of life. Practically speaking, what this means is that domestic animals, and fields and forests, must be treated with kindness and with a view to their health and flourishing. (Wirzba 2011, p. 135)

Still, Wirzba contends that a sacrificial understanding of eating removes it from the 'realm of violence' in a way that makes it possible for 'animals [to] be eaten in ways that respect their integrity and well-being and that honor God' (Wirzba 2011, p. 136). If animal husbandry is practiced correctly, and founded on 'a caring bond between person and animal', it can be 'a suitable context for the faithful eating of meat' (Wirzba 2011, p. 136).

Wirzba's reflections constitute a profound theological account of the act of eating, but when it comes to the ethics of eating animals, there are problems. Perhaps the main one is that we have little reason to think that the killing of sentient creatures is necessary for life. To show that something is necessary is a standard way of showing that it cannot be morally wrong – that's why this claim is important. But why we should agree with it? It is unquestionable that the evolution of life on earth has, in fact, involved the killing of an uncountable number of sentient creatures. It is also clear that some creatures have the form they do today only because their ancestors killed and ate other creatures. But these observations are about how things are, and there is no straightforward route from these observations to the claim that this is how things had to be. This point is explored further in 3.2.2. Moreover, even if it were the case that the only way for God to create complex life was through a violent process of evolution, so that the violence, pain, and suffering we observe in nature were inescapable, that would not establish that we sapiens have to eat animals in order to live or flourish. And as we've already seen, the large number of sapiens living and flourishing without consuming animals shows that claim to be false.

So, we have reasons to doubt the cogency of Wirzba's theological rational-isation of eating animals on its own terms. Once again, however, the point is that even if Wirzba's rejection of vegetarianism succeeded on its own terms, it provides no way to maintain that it is permissible to eat pigs and cows but wrong to eat cats and dogs.

2.4 Conclusion

The dilemma I posed in 2.2 was this: we have every reason to think that pigs and cows deserve as much moral consideration as cats and dogs; therefore, if it is wrong to eat cats and dogs, it is also wrong to eat pigs and cows. None of the theological rationales for eating animals considered provide reason for thinking we might be justified in treating pigs and cows differently to cats and dogs on this issue. As such, if we wish to endorse one of the theological defences of eating animals surveyed above, consistency demands that we judge it morally permissible to eat cats and dogs. Alternatively, if we hold fast to our judgement that it is morally wrong to eat cats and dogs, consist-ency requires us to maintain that it is morally wrong to eat pigs and cows, from which it follows that the theological defences of eating animals considered above are unsuccessful.

3 Evolutionary Violence and the Character of God

Why should they, too, furnish material to enrich the soil for the harmony of the future?

Ivan Karamazov, in Fyodor Dostoyevsky's *The Brothers Karamazov*.

3.1 The Problem

The classical framing of the problem of evil derives from Epicurus, whose statement of the problem is known through its quotation by the third-century Christian theologian Lactantius:

God either wishes to take away evils and cannot, or he can and does not wish to, or he neither wishes nor is able, or he both wishes to and is able. If he wishes to and is not able, he is feeble. . . . If he is able to and does not wish to, he is envious. . . . If he both wishes to and is able, which alone is fitting to god, . . . why does he not remove them? (Lactantius 1965, pp. 92–93)

Some scholars think the problem is especially difficult for Christianity because Christians affirm not only that God is wholly good but that God is Love itself – a love the nature of which is revealed through Jesus Christ's self-sacrifice on the Cross. From the beginning of the tradition, Christians, sensitive to the depth of the challenge, have offered a variety of responses purporting to show how the existence of evil is consistent with the existent of an all-powerful, all-knowing, wholly good God.

Findings from geology, evolutionary biology, and cognitive ethology have, however, sharpened the problem of evil in several ways.[18] First, science has confirmed that many non-human animals suffer and has 'stretched the extent of that suffering over millions and millions of years and millions of species, most of them now extinct' (Southgate 2008b, p. 2). Part of the problem is predation, ubiquitous in nature. Predation brings with it, most obviously, the suffering and premature death of the prey, and any young dependant on the prey animal. But predators themselves are not free from suffering. Some prey animals are able to mount a formidable defence, with the potential to inflict serious injury, even death, on the predator. Moreover, success rates in hunting are usually low and surviving past infancy far from assured. For instance, only about 20% of lion cubs make it to adulthood (Ward 2022, Ch 7, §1), with some of those who don't make it suffering slow deaths due to exposure or starvation. Another part of the problem is parasitism, where one organism lives on or in another organism, typically causing the host organism harm, sometimes death. The scale of parasitism is hard to comprehend. But it is not unlikely that 'every second of every day, hundreds of millions of animals suffer the excruciating agony of being eaten alive' (Esvelt 2019). The natural world, we are learning, contains 'a profusion of horrors' (Schneider 2021a, p. 156).

Predation and parasitism embody an almost universal feature of biological life, namely, that it involves a battle for scarce resources that produces in creatures 'a ruthless egotism which asserts the right on the part of the individual or the species to live at the expense of others' (Williams 1924, p. 520). Various species have hit on the 'profligate recipe' of producing 'extra' young, an 'extravagant and wasteful' strategy that increases the chances of at least some young surviving (Attenborough 1990, pp. 14, 16). A side effect is that 'the majority of [these young] die from disease, starvation, injury, exposure, or predation shortly after birth ... [with] either a quick and painful death, or a slow and painful death' (Johansen, as cited in Crummett 2022, p. 815). The self-assertion and striving, as well as the violence, pain, and suffering they produce, are essential to the evolutionary process – they are 'inscribed' into the

---

[18] There is wide agreement on this, but for a dissenting voice, see Kojonen (2024).

way our world functions (Schneider 2021a, p. 42ff). This should not be surprising since '[e]volution by natural selection cares nothing for the single life' but only for the type (Esvelt 2019), a point not obviated by the fact that some species form mutually beneficial partnerships. As Ryan McLaughlin observes, the world is 'a place of egregious and gratuitous suffering', and this raises 'severe questions concerning the nature of the Creator' (McLaughlin 2019, p. 327).

The second way that evolutionary theory sharpens the problem is by revealing that the world contained violence, suffering, and pain long before the existence of *Homo sapiens*. It follows that such suffering and pain cannot be the result of human sin. If evolutionary violence, pain, and suffering aren't a result of human sin, then there appear to be two options: either violence, pain, and suffering are part of God's untainted, good creation or they are the result of a *cosmic fall* – the fall of some non-human agency. Christopher Southgate has said that this is a 'key fault-line in theology's response to Darwinism' (Southgate 2011, p. 378).

Among those who reject the idea of a cosmic fall are Arthur Peacocke (1993), Holmes Rolston III (1994, 2018), Patricia Williams (2001), Christopher Southgate (2008b, 2011, 2018), Bethany Sollereder (2019), and John Schneider (2021a).

Thinkers who defend a cosmic fall include N. P. Williams (1924), C. S. Lewis (1940), T. F. Torrance (1981, Ch 4), Andrew Linzey (1994), Michael Lloyd (1998), Neil Messer (2009), and Nicola Hoggard Creegan (2013).

3.2 Theodicy without a Cosmic Fall

3.2.1 Only-Way Evolutionary Theodicies

Perhaps the most common type of evolutionary theodicy is the *only-way theodicy*. The key to this theodicy is the claim that the *only way* for God to create free, rational, creative beings capable of entering into loving relationships is through an evolutionary process involving violence, pain, and suffering. Put differently, a violent evolutionary process was *necessary* for the creation of free, rational, creative beings capable of love.

The label 'only-way theodicies' is unfortunate because, as we shall see, almost all theodicies rely on an *only-way* or *necessity* claim, the general form of which is: the only way that God can realise goal *G* is by realising *X*, and realising *X* brings with it the possibility (or actuality) of evil. All such claims aim to justify God by establishing that, given the goal, God had no choice but to cause or allow evil.

What motivates only-way claims is a commitment, often only implicit, to what John Schneider calls the Necessity Condition, according to which 'a morally good person seeks to minimise evil wherever possible, and so only permits it when necessary' (Schneider 2021a, p. 7). Applied to the realm of theodicy, it follows from the Necessity Condition that God is justified in causing evil only if God could not create without it.

Christopher Southgate has developed one of the most thoroughly worked out versions of this approach. He formulates the only-way claim in various ways:

> [C]ertain values can only arise in the biosphere through an evolutionary process ... this was the only, or at least the best, process by which creaturely values of beauty, diversity, and sophistication could arise. (Southgate 2008b, pp. 47–48)

> [E]volution was the only way God could give rise to creaturely selves. (Southgate 2011, p. 387)

> A Darwinian world was the only way to give rise to beauty, diversity, and complexity in creation. (Southgate 2011, p. 387)

> [A] world evolving by natural selection, and therefore necessarily involving the suffering of sentient creatures, is the only sort of world in which the values represented by complex and diverse life could arise. (Southgate 2014, p. 804)

Such claims are supported by the observation that '[t]here is a necessary correlation between the values to which the evolutionary process gives rise and the disvalues of suffering and extinction' (Southgate 2008b, p. 47). This is because, as Arthur Peacocke writes, 'pain, suffering and death are present in biological evolution, as a necessary condition for survival of the individual and transition to new forms' (Peacocke 1993, p. 68). Bethany Sollereder puts it like this: 'the suffering and death of individuals ... drives the development of skill, complexity, and new forms of life through evolution' (Sollereder 2019, p. 183). Broadening the point, Southgate notes that it is 'the same processes – tectonics, creaturely decay, mutation, natural selection, to name only a few – that generate the suffering as also generate the beauty, ingenuity, and diversity of the world of creatures' (Southgate 2017, p. 154). It follows, in the words of Patricia Williams, that '[i]f the universe is to have the goods it does, evil cannot be abolished' (Williams 2001, p. 179). The sciences, then, and evolutionary biology in particular, teach us that those things we value most (life, complexity, creativity, beauty) are deeply intertwined with those things we consider evil (violence, pain, suffering).

To this point is added the observation that the physical, chemical, and biological processes that give rise to evolution predate human beings by millions of years. For almost all thinkers, on both sides of Southgate's fault line, this 'negates Christianity's traditional solution to [the problem of evil]', namely, the appeal to an original human sin which corrupted a perfect creation (Williams 2001, p. 159). The 'scientific record of the Earth's long history before the advent of human beings calls into profound question any account that regards human sin as the cause of struggle and suffering in the nonhuman creation in general' (Southgate 2008b, p. 28).

More than that, only-way theorists suggest that, since we have every reason to think that the structure of the natural world as we observe it today is how the world has always been, we should conclude that the evolutionary processes in their entirety – including the violence and suffering they produce – are the work of God. Sollereder highlights the biblical grounds for this view, noting that God 'claims even the violent and dangerous elements as divine masterpieces' (Sollereder 2019, p. 36). The world as we observe it, 'inclusive of pain and suffering ... is God's "very good" world' (Sollereder 2019, p. 183). On this picture, God is a God of violent means, but that's okay because violence was the only way God could create complexity, beauty, freedom, and love. Some attempt to argue that, in light of the benefits that evolutionary violence brings, we should refuse to consider the violence, pain, and suffering in the natural world evil (Sollereder 2019, p. 185).

The only-way claim is *the* key plank in theodicies which employ it, but few of those who advance an only-way theodicy think it suffices. Two additions that are frequently appealed to are (i) God's presence to individuals who suffer, and (ii) God's redemption of nature.

The idea that God is present to each creature in its suffering is motivated by the goodness of God and grounded in the doctrine of divine immanence. As Jay McDaniel sees it, God's perfect empathy 'does not watch creatures from afar, observing their behavior as from a distance; it feels creatures from their own point of view' (McDaniel 1989, p. 29). For Sollereder, God's goodness means that God will be 'present in the blood and struggle, experiencing the full effects of God's creative intent' (Sollereder 2019, p. 184). This is supposed to help with the idea that God caused this suffering.

The idea that God will redeem the natural world can be worked out in a variety of ways. In the theological tradition, the most prominent meaning of redemption is rescue from a state of sin, in which case it applies almost exclusively to sapiens (see Section 4 for more on this). But as McDaniel explains, redemption might also mean 'freedom from what distresses or harms, contribution to lives beyond one's own, and transformation into an improved state of existence' (McDaniel 1989, p. 42). Holmes Rolston seems to endorse the second notion of redemption in the context of evolution, making the point that in our evolutionary world, 'renewed life comes by blasting the old' (Rolston 1994, pp. 220–221); poetically, '[t]he cougar's fang has carved the limbs of the fleet-footed deer, and vice versa' (Rolston, as cited in Southgate 2008b, p. 2). Famously, Rolston introduced into the literature the case of the second or backup pelican chick. The backup chick serves as insurance for the pelican parents, is usually pushed out of the nest by the first chick, prevented from re-entry by its parents, and, 'nine times out of ten, thrashes about in search of food and then dies of abuse or starvation' (McDaniel 1989, p. 19). Rolston noted that the backup pelican chick is an 'innocent sacrificed to preserve a line, a blood sacrifice perishing that others might live' (Rolston, as cited in McDaniel 1989, p. 43). We might think that the chick's 'life is "redeemed" inasmuch as he acquires this instrumental value for myriad other creatures' (McDaniel 1989, p. 43). Yet many, including McDaniel, do not think this would justify God in the creation of the chick because redemption here amounts to the chick being treated as a means to an end which only benefits others.

McDaniel explores the possibility that the chick might experience redemption in the sense of being transformed into an improved state of existence. For creatures such as the backup pelican chick, this can only be achieved in some form of pelican heaven where the chick will have the chance to 'respond to redemptive possibilities offered by God' (McDaniel 1989, p. 45). Southgate concurs: because 'a God of loving relationship could never regard any creature as a mere evolutionary expedient', we should conclude that God will compensate those creatures who have experienced suffering and pain during their earthly lives (Southgate 2008b, p. 16). This compensation needs to be for the creature itself, and so must involve a heavenly existence where they can experience divine love. Sollereder agrees and stresses that in having a chance to flourish, each creature will also contribute to the flourishing of others: '[t]he second pelican chick will be given a new life that not only gives it a chance to flourish, but that also creates meaning in the lives of those to whom it is in relationship' (Sollereder 2019, p. 157).

3.2.2 A Dilemma for the Only-Way-Based Theodicies

The literature on only-way theodicies contains valuable theological insights, and in this short work, a thorough assessment is not possible. I aim in what follows at a deeper rather than a broader engagement. To that end, I focus on what I take to be the two most problematic aspects of only-way based theodicies.

The first problem can be stated in the form of a dilemma: either the only-way claim involves *absolute* or *metaphysical* necessity, in which case it can do the work required of it in a theodicy, but looks to be false; alternatively, the only-way claim involves *relative* or *restricted* necessity, in which case it is a highly plausible claim, but it cannot do the work required of it by a theodicy.

It is useful to begin by stepping back and considering how the only-way (necessity) claim is supposed to function. The reason almost all theodicies employ some only-way or necessity claim is that if something is necessary, then one has no choice about it, and if one has no choice about it, one cannot be morally blameworthy for it: necessity precludes blameworthiness because by precluding choice it precludes freedom.

There are different types of necessity, and they constrain different types of agents. We sapiens are constrained to some degree by the laws of physics and chemistry, our biological make-up, our historical circumstances, the current state of our technology, and so on. The God of monotheism is not bound by such things. If we take monotheism seriously, for a necessity claim to impose a constraint on God, it must involve absolute or metaphysical necessity.

In his earlier writings, Southgate saw this very clearly: the only-way claim must be grounded in a constraint that 'coexist[s] with God from eternity'; it 'must be a logical necessity if it is to be a constraint on the power of the sovereign Lord' (Southgate 2014, p. 804); it must parallel the necessity in a statement such as 'Necessarily, $2 + 2 = 4$' since only claims involving logical necessity can bind God (Southgate 2017, p. 157).

But here a problem arises: if we are committed to the idea (as Southgate is) that God is the sovereign creator God of Christian monotheism, we don't have much reason to think that the only-way claim construed in terms of absolute necessity is true. If God is the sovereign creator of all that is not God, then God's creative act encompasses the physical laws, the nature of matter, the way chemicals interact, the structure of biological processes, and so on. God could have created a different type of matter subject to different laws. For traditional monotheists, it is not absolutely necessary that matter has the character it does, nor that the laws are what they are. Things are different for, say, process theists. Process theists do not think that God created the world out of nothing. For them, God's creative act consists of *working with something already given* in an attempt to bring about God's goals. Process theists can maintain that the laws of nature, the structure of matter, the way biological systems operate, and so on, constrain or bind God. Traditional monotheists cannot. As Schneider observes, 'it seems implausible on its face that [for] an omnipotent and omniscient God ... no non-Darwinian way of world making was open to God'; theists should 'raise eyebrows' at such a suggestion (Schneider 2021a, pp. 7, 110).

Southgate is candid about being unable to demonstrate that the constraint carries the force of absolute necessity (Southgate 2017, p. 157). Still, he insists:

> It is hard to imagine ... a chemistry for life fundamentally different from the one we know on earth. It is hard to imagine an evolutionary process in which natural selection is not a very significant factor. (Southgate 2017, p. 157)

This doesn't provide a response to the problem, however, because even if Southgate is right about these things being *hard to imagine*, that is not relevant to the point at hand. *Imaginability* is an epistemic notion, and what is imaginable changes over time. Philosophers and theologians used to find it unimaginable that the planets moved in elliptical orbits. Theologians used to think it unimaginable that God would create a species only to let it go extinct. People used to find it unimaginable that complex life could arise from simpler forms without an intelligent designer. These things, once unimaginable, are now taught in school.

In another passage Southgate writes:

> Here is a constraint that seems to coexist with God from eternity, so for the philosophical theologian it is problematic. Surely God could have made creaturely beauty and diversity out of any materials and processes God liked? Whereas for anyone trained in the natural sciences it is a very plausible constraint ... the only way this type of life ... is via Darwinian natural selection, driven by competition, predation, and extinction. (Southgate 2011, pp. 387–388)

The idea here seems to be that there is a genuine constraint, but it's plausibility only becomes apparent to those with sufficient scientific training. However, *pace* Southgate, I do not think that the philosophical theologian and the scientist are disagreeing about the plausibility of the constraint; rather, they are talking about different constraints. The scientist is considering the claim, 'Holding fixed the actual laws of nature and the nature of matter, it's necessary that creaturely beauty and freedom arise through a process involving violence and suffering'. By contrast, the philosophical theologian is considering the claim, 'Holding fixed the laws of logic and any metaphysically necessary truths, it is necessary that creaturely beauty and freedom arise through a process involving violence and suffering'.

The distinction between these two claims brings us to the second horn of the dilemma outlined at the beginning of this section. The claim the scientist is focused on is a claim about *relative* or *restricted* necessity. Relative necessity involves holding fixed facts which are not themselves necessary, and then asking what necessarily follows from them. In this case, the facts we hold fixed are the actual laws, the structure of matter, the way earthly biology works, and perhaps more. Understood in this way, as involving a type of necessity *relative to* these things, the only-way claim is highly plausible. And in his more recent work, Southgate has indicated that he now thinks the only-way claim should be understood in terms of relative necessity (Southgate 2023, p. 35). However, we've already encountered the problem with this: relative necessity doesn't constrain the monotheistic God of Christian theism. Yes, *given* the actual laws of nature, the nature of matter, and so on, it may be that the only way to create life, beauty, and freedom is with a violent evolutionary process. But God is not *given* the laws of nature. God creates the laws. And God could have created them differently.

The only-way theorist thus faces a choice: construe the only-way claim in terms of absolute or metaphysical necessity, in which case the necessity is of the right modality to work in a theodicy, but the claim is highly implausible; or, construe the only-way claim in terms of relative necessity, in which case it is very plausible, but not up to the task of theodicy. Since the only-way claim is usually *the* key plank in this approach to theodicy, this casts serious doubt on the adequacy of the approach.

It may be thought unfair to subject only-way theodicies to this sort of philosophical critique given that those who propose them are (usually) theologians writing for the Christian community, and who are not aiming to provide philosophical analyses of the only-way claim and typically maintain, as we find in Southgate, that 'we are not in a position to be at all definite about this'; instead, these theodicies are offered as 'reasonable, scientifically-informed theological guess[es]' in the hope that they may useful to those already part of a faith community (Southgate 2018, p. 302).[19]

Yet nothing about the project of exploring and offering theological possibilities should exempt the proposals from philosophical assessment. Those who advance no-fall, only-way-based theodicies are admirably committed to the project of developing a theology that coheres well with everything we learn from the sciences. Such thinkers are not shy in taking to task theologians who endorse fall-based theodicies on the grounds that the fall theorists do not take scientific findings seriously enough. They push this criticism even when fall-based theodicies are only put forward as 'reasonable, theological guesses'. This is legitimate. But just as we should require our tentative theological speculations to cohere well with the scientific evidence, so we should require them to stand up to philosophical critique.

3.2.3 Only-Way Theodicies and the Goodness of God

All theologies which refuse to explain evil by appealing to a fall risk making God the author of evil (Williams 1924, p. 534). Put slightly differently, no-fall

---

[19] This line of response was raised by an anonymous referee.

theodicies face the challenge of explaining how we can make sense of God's goodness given that God is 'solely responsible for the existence of the created world' (Southgate 2008b, p. 21, cf. 35), and thus that evolutionary violence is part of God's creation, a direct result of 'the *fiat* of God' (Southgate 2008b, p. 33). Indeed, the fact that evolutionary violence, pain, and suffering are on these views the means God uses to create entails that they have 'a more direct place in the divine will than if they are seen as a strange and unwanted aberration' (Lloyd 1998, p. 151). God, in short, is a God of violent means, the cause and apparent author of evil, 'the ultimate utilitarian' who 'ordains a system requiring the gruesome sacrifice of countless innocents for some greater good' (McLaughlin 2019, p. 332).

Unlike Southgate (2008b, p. 30), I do not think this worry disappears for those who think violence is necessary to create. Even if we accept that (say) robust forms of creativity or freedom can only be produced through a violent evolutionary process, God still had options available. For one, God could have created a world without any life. Such a world would have had various forms of intrinsic value and beauty, even if it didn't contain autonomous creatures. Perhaps more controversially, I think that proponents of only-way claims should also concede that, without using violence, God could have created (for example) a non-evolving world containing perhaps just a single type of very simple life-form, one in harmony with the environment that supports it. Such a world would be much less dynamic and have far fewer types of value than the actual world, but it would have some types of value, and would be free from those disvalues that derive from evolution. Even if only-way theorists reject this last point, it should be stressed that according to traditional Christian theism, God had the option of not creating anything at all. Creation, traditional Christianity supposes, is the result of a free act of God, a free gift. And God would have done no wrong had God decided not to create. Thus, even proponents of evolutionary only-way claims must accept that God had *some* options available. Yet, despite having these options, God decided to create using violence, pain, and suffering. The presence of these options supports the claim that God fully intends the violence of evolution, and so the claim God is their cause and author.

Some only-way theorists attempt to resist this conclusion by appealing to the notion of autonomous creaturely agency as a way of distancing God from evil. For this to work, we need an 'overall vision of the "responsiveness" and "resistance" of creation to the Spirit of God' (Fiddes, as cited in Southgate 2008b, p. 60). For if creaturely resistance to the will of God has some measure of independence from God, then we open the possibility of saying that God created systems that produced the *possibility* of evil, but it was creaturely actions that *realised* that evil.

This will only be possible if we endorse a metaphysic according to which God limits God's own activity and knowledge so that creatures act with genuine independence from God. Created agency and freedom must be construed as incompatible with God's determining action. This does not imply that God is not always and everywhere active as sustaining cause. But it does imply that, with respect to the actions in question, it is *either* creaturely agency *or* divine agency (but not both) that settles what comes to pass. Writers such as John Polkinghorne (1991, p. 43), Arthur Peacocke (1993), and Patricia Williams (2001, pp. 143–144) have all recognised the role incompatibilism plays here. As Peacocke explains:

> [W]e come to regard God's omniscience and omnipotence as 'self-limited' . . . in order that the universe should be of a certain kind – namely, capable through its open-endedness and flexibility of generating complexity, consciousness and freedom. (Peacocke 1993, p. 126)

Given this view, we can say that God does not cause evil, nor is God the author of evil; instead, God *allows* or *permits* evil. This approach is one of the best available routes for no-fall theorists to block the inference that God is the author of evil. One challenge it faces is whether creaturely agency is capable of bestowing ultimate responsibility for evil on creatures. Most thinkers have concluded it is, and this is certainly the historical position of the Christian church. But Marilyn McCord Adams (1999) has argued that human agency is too fragile to secure such a transfer of responsibility, and if this is true of sapien agency, it will also be true for the other forms of created agency on earth.

Only-way theorists who reject incompatibilism between creaturely freedom and autonomy and God's determining activity will be unable to explain how creatures who are caused to do exactly what they do by God's sufficient causation can possess an autonomy that distances God from what the creatures do. Southgate *may* fall into this group – he thinks incompatibilism is 'question-able', and appears to endorse critiques of the idea that creaturely freedom and divine agency are a zero-sum game (Southgate 2008b, pp. 58, 158) – but it is in the end unclear. Whether or not Southgate falls into this camp, the point is that without incompatibilism, God determines all. And if God determines all, creaturely 'resistance' just is God bringing it about that the creature resist. This view cannot make sense of a genuine creaturely response because every detail of the creature's action is settled by God and only God. There is, on this view, no way to identify certain events as things that God merely allowed, but did not cause. God is the cause and author of all.

It seems that this latter position – only-way theodicy without incompatibilism – can only be reconciled with the goodness of God if we weaken our conception of divine goodness. Interestingly, this is something that some no-fall theorists are willing to countenance. Southgate, for instance, says he is 'happy to admit that the only way argument constrains our sense not only of divine omnipotence but also of omnibenevolence' (Southgate 2018, p. 303).[20] There's much to explore here, but what should be clear already is that, even if the only-way claim itself were rendered plausible, only-way theodicies become workable only if we weaken our conception of divine goodness.

3.2.4 An Aesthetic Evolutionary Theodicy

While most advocates of no-fall theodicies agree that some sort of only-way claim is essential for any viable theodicy, some disagree. Drawing from the work of Roderick Chisholm, John Schneider proposes that instead of the Necessity Condition, 'God's only moral obligation in authorizing evil is to meet the Defeat Condition'. The Defeat Condition states that God is justified in allowing an evil if God *defeats* that evil. And an evil is said to be defeated when it is 'integrated as a constitutive part of a valuable composite whole that not only outweighs the evil, but could not be as valuable as it is *without the evil*' (Schneider 2021a, pp. 8, 7). This benefits the theodicist because on this view, 'God is not good in that meticulous moral manner' required by the Necessity Condition; instead, God is free to maximise 'goodness, truth, and beauty even at great cost to creatures', free to '[use] evil, including the suffering of creatures, as instrumental means to these valuable cosmic ends' (Schneider 2021a, pp. 8–9).

To explain this, Schneider presents an *aesthetic theodicy*, the central idea of which is that we can liken God to a cosmic artist. Artists sometimes incorporate elements of ugliness or discord into their works in ways that result in the ugliness or discord contributing to the positive value of the completed work. This is possible because the aesthetic value of an art work is not an additive function of the value of its parts; rather, the value of the whole derives from its organic unity. Adams cites the bilious green in Monet's depiction of Rouen cathedral and the discordant notes in Stravinsky's *Rite of Spring* as examples (Adams 1999, p. 149).

Proponents of aesthetic theodicies suggest that God's activity can be construed in such terms: God's causing or allowing of an evil in creation may be analogous to the artist's using something ugly to increase the overall aesthetic value, since, so we might think, God can incorporate the evil into the organic unity of the cosmos in a manner which increases its beauty and moral value.

---

[20] It should be noted that Southgate does not concede that genuine creaturely autonomy requires incompatibilism. Kittle (2022) provides further defence of incompatibilism.

There is theological precedent for this sort of *aesthetic theodicy*. Augustine and others held something like an aesthetic view. These writers expressed an 'aesthetic optimism', taking for granted that the universe exhibits overwhelming order, harmony, and beauty, so much so that even the evil of those suffering eternal conscious torment in hell was a 'necessary element in the artistic composition of the world' (Harnack 1898, p. 115). Schneider acknowledges that the 'appeal to the beauty of harmony, balance, and the integration of all parts into a pleasing whole barely applies to the natural realm as unveiled by evolutionary science'; indeed, the very opposite is the case, because evolutionary biology has 'unveiled' to us the dysteleological phenomena of mass extinctions, anti-cosmic 'monsters' (viruses, parasites, and so forth), and violence 'inscribed' into the fabric of the universe (Schneider 2021a, pp. 163, 3–5). Moreover, Schneider agrees that Augustine's contention that hell adds to the beauty of God's cosmic artwork is morally objectionable. Such views allow putative general goods to trample the interests of individual sufferers; as Adolf von Harnack wrote, '[t]he individual and evil are lost to view in the notion of beauty' (1898, p. 114).

Schneider's aesthetic view differs in three significant ways. First, he holds 'that God approves the existence of elemental Chaos within the Cosmos', that 'God has included Chaos in the cosmic design' and 'values the inclusion of this anti-cosmic presence in the world as a good thing' (Schneider 2021a, pp. 183–184). Schneider defends this idea by presenting a reading of the book of Job, according to which it develops the idea of the 'messianic sublime' – an aesthetic vision that sees God bringing about a beautiful cosmos in and through violence (Schneider 2021a, p. 192).

Second, Scheider supplements the aesthetic he finds in Job with the idea that the natural world, with its myriad processes where suffering and death give rise to new life, can be understood as in some sense *kenotic*. This is an idea we find in Rolston, Peacocke, Southgate and others. Rolston thinks the natural world is cruciform because 'like Christ, some animals sacrifice themselves so that other animals might live and flourish' (Schneider 2021a, pp. 202–203). Southgate adds that the cruciform character of animal life is valuable for its moral symbolism. Schneider agrees, and maintains that the activate participation of creatures in 'the "kenotic" creative life-giving evolutionary process' is in itself a 'very great moral good' (Schneider 2021a, p. 204).

Third, instead of proposing that the beauty of the cosmos as a whole suffices to defeat particular evils, Schneider holds that divine goodness requires that God defeat each evil *for the individual who has suffered it*. It is evident, of course, that many creatures suffer great evils which are not defeated during the creature's antemortem existence. As such, Schneider, like others who endorse this requirement, maintains that God will defeat such evils in an afterlife.

Schneider's work contains many thought-provoking and challenging ideas and is a robust defence of an aesthetic theodicy. The summary I've just presented does not do justice to the depth of Schneider's position but it does, I hope, outline enough of the fundamentals to allow me to articulate what I think will be the main sticking points for Scheider's approach.

3.2.5 The Necessity in Defeat

The first issue to raise is that the Defeat Condition may not be so neatly separable from the Necessity Condition as Schneider supposes. Consider one of Chisholm's examples of the defeat of evil: the defeat of fear by courage (Chisholm 1990, p. 60). It is possible for courage to defeat fear because the positive value of a person's courage may outweigh the badness of their fear *and* the value of that courage is in part *constituted by* the fear: courage is only possible given fear. It therefore follows that the value of the whole could not be good in the way it is *without* the evil part (Schneider 2021a, p. 72).

But here we face an interesting question: if the whole didn't contain the fear, it wouldn't contain the courage, so which whole is it, exactly, that 'could not be as good' as the one containing the fear and the courage? If there were a composite whole exactly like the actual one, only instead of containing the fear and the courage which defeats that fear, it contained an experience akin to and as valuable as courage, but one which didn't involve any fear, that would seem to be a whole as valuable as the fear-and-courage whole. And we should, following Chisholm, be tempted to say that God should have created that instead (Chisholm 1990, p. 68).

If that is right, then what's doing the justificatory work is not defeat alone but defeat combined with the fact that *there is no way to obtain the positive value obtained other than by the defeat of evil*. But this means there is an only-way claim – or a set of only-way claims – at the heart of Schneider's aesthetic theodicy.

This is important not because Schneider explicitly repudiates only-way claims but because it affects the plausibility of aesthetic theodicies. One of the supposed benefits of an aesthetic theodicy is that it sets God free to maximise 'goodness, truth, and beauty even at great cost to creatures'. But if what justifies the causing of evil is that the evil is defeated *and* that the *evil is necessary* to secure a certain type of positive value, then moving to an artistic analogue may not realise much more freedom for God than otherwise was the case. God is free to '[use] evil, including the suffering of creatures, as instrumental means to these valuable cosmic ends' (Schneider 2021a, pp. 8–9), but only in cases where the evil and its defeat are the *only way to obtain the good* thereby produced. So the aesthetic perspective may not be quite as beneficial as it first appeared.

3.2.6 Analogical Breakdown

Central to Schneider's theodicy is the idea that we can envisage God as a cosmic artist, and it cannot be doubted that Schneider develops this view with sophistication. We can straightforwardly agree, I think, that when it comes to art, the value of the whole can be increased by the inclusion of ugliness or discord in just the way described by Chisholm and Adams. We can also agree with Adams (1999, pp. 132ff) that aesthetic qualities are by no means irrelevant to morality.

Still, none of this establishes that it is legitimate to think of God as a cosmic artist free to ignore the Necessity Condition. Schneider, drawing from Job and kenotic theory, describes a 'wild' God engaged in the project of crafting a beautiful cosmos from the midst of chaos. But while Schneider might present a good biblical case for the legitimacy of the analogy, he doesn't adequately address the apparent points of disanalogy.

The first point of disanalogy is that neither ugliness nor discord are *evil*. Thus, simply to observe that artists incorporate *ugliness* or *discord* into works of art in a way that increases the work's beauty does not yet show that it may be possible to incorporate *evil* into a whole so as to increase the whole's moral value or aesthetic value. We might note here that the parallel doesn't seem to work with what is sometimes considered the third transcendental, truth: it isn't possible to incorporate a falsehood into a work of theory in a way which allows the theory as a whole to 'defeat' the falsehood, producing a theory which is truer than it could have been without the falsehood.

A more significant point of disanalogy is that works of art do not involve the artist making use of living, sentient creatures who are the source of intrinsic value. Patches of ugly, bilious green paint do not have needs, or desires, or interests that can be thwarted. Patches of ugly, bilious green paint are not moral subjects. Living, sentient creatures do have needs, desires, and interests. And they are moral subjects. The intrinsic value of a patch of ugly, bilious green paint – let's accept for the sake of argument that it may have some intrinsic value – is qualitatively different to the intrinsic value of a living, sentient being, and on multiple counts.

These two points of disanalogy give substantive reason to think that, even if we conceive of God as a cosmic artist, we would need to say a lot more before concluding that God has the kind of moral license possessed by the human artist creating a work of art. And Schneider's sophisticated biblical case for the analogy doesn't help address these concerns.

Another key part of Schneider's case is the parallel he draws between biological life and God's kenotic self-emptying in the work of Jesus Christ. Schneider leans heavily on this supposed parallel because, in making creaturely suffering akin to God's own suffering in Christ, it bestows increased value on creaturely suffering. This enables one to say that the suffering may have positive value for the suffering creature, and may even be a way for the creature to commune with God.

Here again, however, there is reason to question the success of the analogy. A criticism that has often been pushed against those who construe the natural world as cruciform or kenotic is that, whereas Christ's kenotic act of self-sacrifice was voluntarily willed, the 'sacrifice' made by non-human animals is involuntary. Indeed, except for some special cases, it seems wholly inappropriate to describe non-humans as giving themselves for others. Biological life on earth is characterised not by self-sacrifice but, to quote N. P. Williams again, 'a ruthless egotism which asserts the right on the part of the individual or the species to live at the expense of others' (Williams 1924, p. 520). This is the very opposite of God's self-emptying in the voluntary self-sacrifice of Jesus Christ.

Schneider replies to this worry by arguing that Christ's work was only 'partially voluntary' because Christ 'would have chosen anything other than the humiliatingly nightmarish horror … of death by crucifixion' (Schneider 2021a, p. 207). But it's unclear what this means. Presumably, Christ *would have* chosen differently *had* some alternative set of circumstances been actual. But what relevance does that have? What matters, morally, is what Christ *did* choose given the *actual circumstances*. Perhaps the idea is that Christ had a desire to avoid Golgotha (a desire he didn't act on), and in virtue of that desire, Christ's action was therefore not fully voluntary. But the presence of a desire opposed to the desire one in fact chooses to act on does not undermine the voluntariness of one's decision. If it did, no decision we're ever conflicted about could ever be voluntary.

Moreover, the difference between the action of Christ and the action of non-human animals is much deeper than the applicability or non-applicability of the labels 'voluntary' and 'involuntary' may suggest. The complexity of sapien cognition and volition means that the sense in which human action can be voluntary differs markedly from the sense in which even the action of the most intellectually sophisticated mammals can be voluntary. Thus, even if some non-human animals could be said to voluntarily sacrifice themselves, we'd still want to be hesitant about affirming the analogy.

In response to this sort of worry, Schnieder writes that 'the fact that animal "kenotic" self-sacrifice is involuntary . . . does not invalidate the comparison, for in both kenotic cases, God calls servants to participate in a very great good' (Schneider 2021b). Yet, the idea of God's *calling* non-sapiens is, for creatures incapable of anything even approaching symbolic communication, itself an analogy the cogency of which has not been established. That is, it's opaque what it could mean to say that God calls, say, the white-lipped snail to 'participate in a very great good' – what could such a call consist in?

In sum, the case for a 'striking similarity between the Christian narrative of redemption and the Darwinian story of species' has not yet been convincingly made (Schneider 2021b). There may be a surface similarity, but further inspection gives reason to think that the notion of kenosis is inapplicable to most creaturely activity. Thus, at – literally – the crucial point, the analogy at the heart of Schneider's account breaks down. Animals do not go about sacrificing themselves for the beauty of God's cosmic plan; precisely the opposite: they are sacrificed by God, with no choice in the matter, and no understanding of what is going on.

3.2.7 Aesthetic Theodicies and the Goodness of God

In this section I want to suggest that, even if all of the above objections can be answered, still, on Schneider's view, it is difficult to avoid construing God as the cause and author of evil. Schneider does occasionally refer to God as the 'active cause' of evil, but he 'does not wish bluntly and simply to deem God to be the "direct author of evil"' (Schneider 2021b). Instead, Schneider wants to maintain that God 'indirectly, yet causally, "authorized" the existence of . . . evils . . . by virtue of the randomness of evolution, albeit within constraints' (Schneider 2021b).

Schneider doesn't expand on what he means here, but the idea may be something like the following: if God sets up a system with certain boundaries, a system that can unfold in a variety of ways, some of which are evil, and some not, and if God makes it the case that it is genuinely random which way things unfold, then, if evil does come to pass, there is enough distance between God and evil for us to deny God's authorship of the evil.

Is this the case? Frequently, randomness does interfere with human agency, and in so doing, diminishes our authorship. This is because randomness reduces our knowledge, both of what *will* happen and what *could* happen. But things are otherwise with God. God's position with respect to randomness is more akin to the following scenario: imagine you are tasked with replying to customer support enquires over email. Each email must finish with a closing sentence.

You setup a system which randomly selects one of ten pre-written closing sentences. You wrote all ten closing responses, and you designed and setup the system which randomly picks one. Having just completed an email, you press the button to insert one of the closing sentences – let's say response number 3 is selected. There is a substantial sense in which you own – you are the author of – closing sentence number 3 being incorporated into your email. After all, you created every possibility (and so have full knowledge of the possibility space); you setup the system; you pushed the button. Thus, if you choose to push the button, you are the author of what comes to pass.

Just so, once we're clear that (i) God is the author of the range of available possibilities, and (ii) God is the author of the randomness-employing system which realises one of the possibilities, it becomes apparent that randomness in the actual causal chain does very little, if anything, to diminish divine authorship. So, while Schneider may not want to affirm that God is the author of evil, there is some reason to doubt whether his theodicy has the resources to facilitate this denial. This conclusion becomes all the more compelling when we remember that, according to Schneider, God could have chosen to create without using violence, pain, and suffering but, in full knowledge of the evils it would produce, God chose to create using violence, God formed the intention to create using violence. We can only conclude that God is the author of these evolutionary evils. We have no grounds for saying that God *merely authorised* but *did not author* evil. But, it appears to be deeply morally problematic to affirm that God is the author of evil, even if God defeats the evil God causes, indeed, even if God defeats the evil for those individuals who suffer it.

Schneider's aesthetic theodicy may still be able to reconcile evil with God's goodness. As with those only-way theorists who reject incompatibilism, this may be possible if we significantly weaken our conception of goodness so that goodness is consistent with the intentional authoring of avoidable evil. No doubt there will be stark differences of opinion on how plausible such an understanding of divine goodness is, and whether it does justice to the name, just as there are differences of opinion over whether it is a problem to weaken omniscience in the way required by (say) open theism. All I will add here is that, of all the divine attributes, goodness is probably the one we should be most hesitant to weaken. In the words of Susan Neiman, 'it may be hard to acknowledge God's limits, but it's less frightening than denying God goodwill' (Neiman 2002, p. 20).

3.3 Theodicy with a Cosmic Fall

On the other side of Southgate's key fault-line are those who think that the goodness of God means God cannot be a god of violent means. As T. F. Torrance sees it, 'The Cross of Christ tells us unmistakably that all ... pain, suffering, disease, corruption, death ... are an outrage against the love of God and a contradiction of good order in his creation' (Torrance 1981, p. 139). Such theologians attribute the violence, pain and suffering we observe in the world to an agency or force other than God. Traditionally, of course, that agency was taken to be the first sapiens. This explains how the existence of evil is compatible with the existence of an all-powerful, wholly good God: in creating the first sapiens with free will, God creates *the possibility* that sapiens will misuse their free will, but *the actual* existence of evil is down to sapiens, not God. For this to work, creaturely free will must be construed as being incompatible with causal and divine determinism; only thus do we stand a chance of attributing sin and moral evil to sapiens *and not also to God*. Clearly, this account of evil is a non-starter when it comes to explaining the pain and suffering of the billions upon billions of creatures who existed before the emergence of sapiens. One straightforward modification is to appeal instead to an angelic fall. Alvin Plantinga (1974) notes this as a possibility, and the view finds significant defence by Michael Lloyd (1998). Since an angelic fall can be placed at any arbitrary time, it can serve as the origin of all evil. But aside from having to explain how a temporal angelic sin could disrupt the laws of nature, many think the scientific evidence leaves any appeal to a historical fall untenable.

Neil Messer articulates an alternative that invokes the idea of a *non-historical cosmic fall*. Messer starts with the conviction, deriving from a certain interpretation of Genesis 1–2, Isaiah 11, and other passages, that the 'very good' creation is 'a world of peace and plenty, without predation, struggle, violence or destruction' (Messer 2020, p. 89), a world where creatures 'have all that they need to live and flourish, and no need to kill one another for food' (Messer 2009, p. 141). Given this starting point, Messer must attribute the evil in the world to something other than God. Now, Messer endorses the critique of theodicy advanced by D. Z. Phillips, and so thinks there are severe limits on explanation here: 'If we try to explain how or why this should be, we will inevitably find ourselves facing a mystery' (Messer 2020, p. 89). For Messer, we can say *something*, but what we can say does not function as an *explanation*. Thus, guided by the Christian tradition, we should hold that it is a mistake to 'represent evil as an independent cosmic force opposed to God' (Messer 2020, p. 90). Instead, evil should be thought of as a privation, or a lack of goodness (Messer 2020, p. 91). Messer follows Karl Barth in identifying evil with *nothingness*. Nothingness here 'is not nothing ... but ... is what God rejected, and *did not will* ... it is the chaos, disorder and annihilation that threatens God's creation, and to which God is opposed' (Messer 2009, p. 149). Evolutionary violence is 'opposed to God's creative purpose' and so part of, or a consequence of, this nothingness. Messer acknowledges that the nothingness 'has a strange, paradoxical, negative kind of existence' (Messer 2009, p. 149). Yet, for Messer, we should stop short of attempting to explain things further. Making a move standard among Reformed thinkers, Messer says we should direct our attention instead to what God has done to overcome evil (Messer 2009, pp. 149, 151).

The first point to make when assessing Messer's account is that, just like Southgate's, it depends on an only-way necessity claim that serves to exonerate God. This is worth highlighting because much of the contemporary discussion seems to suppose that those theodicies which suggest that evolutionary violence is the only way God can create beauty, love and freedom are unique in relying on a necessity claim, whereas in fact necessity claims are the cornerstone of all theodicy.[21] What is the only-way claim Messer relies on? There are two options, depending on how we read Messer. On one reading, Messer means to lean very heavily on the idea that evil is a privation or lack. If we take that thought seriously, the nothingness can have no substance of its own, and must be something like an undesirable, negative, systems-level property of the universe God creates. Just as one cannot have a mountain range without at least one valley, where the valley is just a lack or absence of matter, so, the thought might be, one cannot have various types of matter interacting to produce life without a nothingness standing ready to annihilate the created order – this is speculative, of course, since Messer eschews explanation. This reading suffers from at least two objections. First, and as Southgate (2017, p. 155) has recently noted, this reading of Messer comes close to saying that the nothingness is part of the 'logical fabric of the universe', and if so, it aligns Messer's view very closely with Southgate's own. One could think of Messer's description of the nothingness as a re-statement of Southgate's only-way claim, only in more general terms: 'Necessarily, the only way God can create beauty, creativity and freedom is by creating a system with properties that threaten annihilation'. This only-way claim is about as plausible as Southgate's. But, more to the point, this reading makes God the creator of the Nothingness, which is exactly what Messer is trying to avoid. It will be unsatisfactory for anyone who shares Messer's conviction that God's infinite goodness precludes God's untainted creation from containing evil. Second, on this reading Messer's view inherits all the problems that plague the privation view of evil, the most serious being that it cannot explain paradigm cases of evil: the pain experienced due to (say) betrayal is a real, concrete reality, not merely a lack, and attempts to say

---

[21] The exceptions are those theologies which maintain that God is beyond all morality, such that God's causing evil and suffering is not a problem.

otherwise only gain traction by conflating the ontological and teleological understandings of privation.[22]

The second reading of Messer construes the nothingness as some sort of negative agency. Arguably, this is the reading that is required if Messer's account is to be an improvement over Southgate's with respect to preserving God's goodness. If the nothingness has its own agency, then the disorder and chaos in creation can potentially be attributed to this nothingness *and not also to God*. As with traditional fall theologies, the agency's autonomy must be construed as being incompatible with causal and divine determinism; if it weren't, then God would be the ultimate author of all this agency's 'actions' and we'd be no further on. If we take Messer's disavowal of a historical fall seriously, we would have to suppose that this agency was atemporal. We would also have to suppose this agency were so powerful that its rebellion could, contrary to God's wishes, adversely affect the very nature of God's subsequent creation. Once we're clear about these details, we see that this reading just is a version of the angelic fall view.

Compared to Southgate's view and the first reading of Messer, this view, by relying on a substantive created autonomy incompatible with causal and divine determinism, is able to put some distance between God and evil. However, there are significant theological problems. If we posit an atemporal or eternal cosmic force opposed to God we risk falling into Manichean dualism. As Messer states, to posit a force eternally opposed to God 'would be a great mistake, one that mainstream Christian theology has for the most part tried hard to resist' (Messer 2019, p. 339).

It may be possible to avoid this worry if we suppose that the nothingness is, after all, temporal, but the first temporal creation. The rebellion of this agency would need to account for the corrupted character of the whole natural world. This might suggest an incredibly powerful temporal being, or some sort of two-stage creation, where this first created entity bears some sort of mystical unity to the rest of creation, such that it's rebellion can bring about chaos and violence throughout the entire created order. The first might be thought incompatible with monotheism; the second option looks increasingly ad hoc. Additionally, a two-stage creation may risk introducing theological difficulties as far as God's intention for creation is concerned. It's also worth noting that, since the view requires incompatibilism, it is not one that Messer himself could endorse, since he rejects the idea that creaturely freedom is incompatible with God's determining activity. Still, the theist has few options here, and this approach may well

---

[22] See Todd Calder (2007) for details.

be the best route available for developing an account which reconciles God's infinite goodness with evolutionary violence.

In these debates there are clearly significant differences over basic intuitions concerning what, for instance, God's infinite goodness entails. There are also differences in methodological approach, and one way to inch the debate forward may be to focus attention on methodology. Southgate, for instance, doubts whether we can resolve disagreements by appealing to biblical passages because the passages in question 'can be approached from very different strategies in biblical interpretation' (Southgate 2017, p. 156). By contrast, Messer doubts that 'finite and sinful human beings can gain knowledge of God and God's ways from our scientific investigations of the natural world', holding instead that 'genuine knowledge of God and God's ways will depend on God's self-revelation' (Messer 2020, p. 94). It's interesting to note that the theological dogma on which Messer's suspicious-of-reason epistemology is based is itself the product of rational reflection on the apparent universal character of sapien sin (Williams 1924, p. 18ff): recognising the universality of sin, early Jewish and then Christian thinkers sought out passages of scripture to explain the origin of evil, turning first to Genesis 6, and then, when it was realised that this could not explain the pre-diluvian sin, to Genesis 3. All this suggests that critically attending to the sources of our judgements about (e.g.) divine goodness, as well as about which methodologies to employ, may at least clarify where the fundamental disagreements lie, even among theorists who disagree on which methodologies should be employed.

3.4 Summary

In the two preceding sections I have outlined and assessed two of the main approaches to reconciling the existence of the traditional understanding of God with evolutionary violence. Southgate thinks Messer's view is 'profoundly problematic' (Southgate 2017, p. 155), and his assessment seems apt. But Southgate's view relies on a necessity claim that we have every reason to think is false. And on both of the no-fall views considered, Southgate's and Schneider's, God is the cause and, what looks likely, the author, of evil. These two views can reconcile theism will evolutionary violence and the evils it generates only by significantly weakening our understanding of God's goodness. If anything is clear, it's that the believer wishing to stay within the boundaries of traditional theism has precious few options, none particularly good, and each of which carries a significant cost.

That each of the proposed ways of reconciling traditional theism with evil each ends up weakening either divine power or divine goodness suggests that approaches to this problem which explicitly reject the traditional view of God may turn out to be the most satisfactory. It is relatively uncontroversial, for example, that process theology succeeds in placing more distance between God and evil than classical versions of Christianity can achieve. McDaniel (1989) has done important work on the problem of animal pain and suffering from this perspective. Pursuing this thought further, it may simply not be possible to reconcile the idea of a loving, personal God with the all-pervasive violence that exists in nature, even with significant revisions to our concept of God. If so, this may speak in favour of an approach such as Wesley Wildman's (2008b, 2008a), where the Divine or Ultimate is construed as the ground of all reality, but not personal and not good in a 'humanly recognizable way' (and so, not morally good).

Another response would be the rejection of theism altogether. The nature and extent of suffering in the natural world 'seems to call into question the goodness of the God who made this creation', whereas if there is no God, 'the problem resolves itself' (Southgate 2008b, p. 5). Neither Southgate nor Messer take themselves to be answering the problem of animal pain conceived of as an argument for atheism (Southgate 2008b, p. 6; Messer 2009, p. 145). But unless we are going to affirm faith no matter what, in the face of any and all contravening evidence, the severity of the problem and the paucity of plausible options, may lead some to a reluctant agnosticism, even atheism. Such a response could hardly be considered unreasonable. As Creegan writes, 'It is not surprising that the full impact of all of this on thoughtful and sensitive people is often a loss of faith' (Creegan 2013, p. 4).

4 Non-Sapiens, the Image of God, Redemption

Human animality is variously explained, ignored, sublimated, obscured, sacrificed, or negated in order to preserve humanity's unique status before God and basic creaturely integrity. The problem of human animality is an abyss over which theological anthropology has been trained to leap.

Eric Meyer, Inner Animalities, p. 4

4.1 Introduction

There has been an increasing volume of work done on animals within the theological academy over the past forty years but, as detailed in Section 1, the dominant view throughout Christian history, and among religious people today, is that non-human animals are of only marginal theological interest. Many find their relevance to theology baffling. If the topic of animals does arise in a church context, the questions asked often fail to progress much beyond 'Will I see my pet in heaven?', or 'Why did God create the dinosaurs?'.

Yet the idea that animals are of little importance to theology is mistaken, if only because what we know about, for example, bonobos and chimpanzees, not to mention the various extinct species of human, teaches us much about ourselves. Some of the questions animals raise for theology include: What value does God place on animals? What role do animals play in God's purposes? Do any non-human animals reveal the goodness of God? Can any animals experience religiously significant emotions? Do any non-sapiens possess a form of morality, or the capacity to sin? Do any non-sapiens have an immaterial soul? Can any non-human animals become aware of God? Were any members of the other species of human able to become aware of God? Are any non-sapiens made in the image of God? What relevance (if any) does Christ's Incarnation and Resurrection have for non-sapiens? What relevance (if any) does the Atonement have for non-sapiens? How should we think about our own animality, and how does it relate to the moral and religious aspects of sapien life?

It is not easy for us to consider these issues impartially because, as noted in sections 1 and 2, we eat the flesh and wear the skins of many non-humans and so have a vested interest in viewing non-humans a certain way. The practice of rationalising our use and abuse of God's other creatures runs deep in the Christian tradition, and it can be difficult to think ourselves out of the categories and patterns of thought that preclude the questions above from gaining any traction.

This section aims to show the relevance of animals to various areas of Christian doctrine. I begin by comparing the traditional theological understanding of the cosmos with the view presented to us by modern science, to show some of the ways theology has already adapted itself to scientific findings. I then explore how animals may bear on the image of God and the Incarnation.

4.2 The Traditional Theological Worldview

When early Christian thinkers developed their theologies, they largely assumed the Aristotelian-Ptolemaic worldview dominant at the time (van Helden 1985, pp. 16, 37, 40). On this view, the earth was at the centre of the universe, surrounded by a series of solid spheres. Earthly entities, composites of the four terrestrial elements (earth, water, air, and fire), were thought to be 'radically different' to the heavenly bodies inhabiting the celestial realm (the sun, moon, etc), all of which travelled in 'perfect' circular motion and were made of an incorruptible fifth element: *quintessence* or *aether* (Richards 2000, p. 5). Religious scholars thought that heaven, the dwelling place of the elect, angels, and God, was spatially located in the outermost sphere, the *Empyreum* (McDannell and Lang 1990, p. 80ff).[23]

Theological understandings of the human person invariably began with the idea found in Genesis that we sapiens are made in image of God:

> God created humankind in his image, in the image of God he created them; male and female he created them. God blessed them, and God said to them, 'Be fruitful and multiply, and fill the earth and subdue it; and have dominion over the fish of the sea and over the birds of the air and over every living thing that moves upon the earth.' (Genesis 1:27–28, NSRV)

These verses have 'profoundly influenced Western conceptions of human nature and personal identity' (Martin and Barresi 2006, p. 41), and a straight-forward reading suggests that modern humans *and only modern humans* are made in the *imago Dei* – the image of God. That has been how almost all Christian scholars have read this passage. The demarcation between *Homo sapiens* and other animals was thought to be 'strongly drawn, well-marked, and unpassable' (Thomas 1983, p. 35). Even today most theologians presume without argument that Genesis teaches a hard-and-fast distinction between *Homo sapiens* and all other animals (Cunningham 2009, p. 101). A second idea found in this passage – that we modern humans have dominion over other animals – has been and remains a central motif in Western culture. Although humanity's initial dominion was given in Eden, where all creatures were vegan and lived in peace with one another, it is safe to say this point was lost on most commentators until the latter part of the twentieth century, and in any case the force of the point is weakened by God's permitting humans to eat animals in Genesis 9. Many other passages reinforce this anthropocentric interpretation of Genesis. Two examples illustrate this. First, Jesus commanded the Gerasene demon into a herd of pigs who subsequently perished; given that Jesus could have simply vanquished the demons, this appears to demonstrate disregard for the pigs. Such was the view of Augustine, who took this passage to demonstrate that 'we have no moral obligations whatsoever to animals' (Steiner 2010, p. 114). Second, in 1 Corinthians 9, Paul reinterprets Deuteronomy 25:4 so that it teaches, not concern for the animals we use, but the importance of honouring humans with different roles. Paul's reworking was subsequently used by Aquinas and many others in support of anthropocentrism. There are verses that can be interpreted in a way that facilitates an

---

[23] The ancient biblical authors also believed that heaven qua God's dwelling place was spatially located "directly above the earth", though they based this view on a different cosmology; see Gooder (2011, pp. 7–8).

animal-friendly theology,[24] but these minority readings are often strained, and have not featured prominently in the tradition.

The first Christian theologians combined this Bible-inspired view of the human person with a wider metaphysics known today as the *Great Chain of Being* (Lovejoy 2009). According to the latter, everything that exists finds its place in a hierarchy of being, proceeding from the lowliest type of existent, inanimate matter, through plants, animals, to sapiens, and then up through myriad types of spiritual beings, culminating with God. Each being on the Chain, from fungi to fieldmouse, orchid to octopus, is what it is in virtue of its essence. Essences were conceived of as Platonic ideas in the divine mind, and theologians explained that since there was a 'necessity of production inherent in the divine goodness', God's creative act 'inevitably extended to all possible things' so that there were no gaps in the Chain (Lovejoy 2009, pp. 67–68, 69). Moreover, since essences modelled 'the eternal order of the Ideas in the Divine Reason' (Lovejoy 2009, p. 261), and since God was immutable, it followed that the types of entity, and their position in the hierarchy, were static and unchange-able. It was therefore, prior to 1700, inconceivable that humans might produce lasting changes in the natural world (Robertson 2020, Ch 8), and for similar reasons extinction was considered a theological impossibility: John Ray wrote that 'the destruction of any one species' would be a 'dismembering of the universe' that would render it imperfect (Ray 1693, p. 147). Writing in 1693, Ray felt some need to *defend* this view; prior to that, it needed no defence because '[t]he idea that species might become extinct would ... have seemed absurd: why would God have created them only to let them vanish?' (Robertson 2020, §2.3).

We sapiens, situated roughly in the middle of the Chain, represented a 'point of transition from the merely sentient to the intellectual forms of being' (Lovejoy 2009, p. 190), 'the only being that combined heavenly and earthly natures' (Richards 2000, p. 6): bodies made of matter and immaterial souls made of the fifth element. As Janet Richards notes, this cosmology 'both reflected and entrenched the Christian rejection of the material, and its concep-tion of the bodily as sinful' (Richards 2000, pp. 6–7). The angels, God's other rational creatures, had souls but no bodies. Non-human animals, by contrast, had material bodies but no souls, and were therefore the 'lower creatures': able to sense, but without thought or intellect. On pain of contradiction, this view cannot hold that animal behaviour is the result of abstraction, inference, prob-lem solving or anything else requiring cognition. Animal behaviour was instead considered the result of 'divinely implanted instinct' (Thomas 1983, p. 34).

---

[24] See Kemmerer (2012, Ch 6) for a good overview.

Significantly, because we sapiens were the only earthly creatures who possessed immaterial souls, we were considered the pinnacle of God's earthly realm. The idea that the image of God consists in possessing a soul that bestows a faculty of reason is known today as the *substantive* or *structural* account of the image of God. It has been by far '[t]he most prevalent way of understanding the image of God throughout history' (Cortez 2010, p. 18). Joshua Farris makes a good case that theology has had a 'long and sustained commitment to a dogmatic package that ties the *imago Dei* to the soul' (Farris 2021, pp. 311, 316).

Theologians considered the supremacy of sapiens 'central to the Divine plan', and there developed the belief that all other entities, including animals, 'were not made for themselves, but for the use and service of man' (Thomas 1983, pp. 18–19; Lovejoy 2009, p. 186). Keith Thomas outlines how, on this basis, almost everyone agreed that killing animals for pleasure was lawful; some Christians argued that it justified bear baiting and cock-fighting (Thomas 1983, pp. 19, 22). In medieval England cock-fights were held in churchyards 'with the full approval of the incumbent', and in Wales church bells were often sounded in honour of the winner (Turner 1964, pp. 36, 57). Theologians and preachers would routinely claim such things as: 'the instinct which brought fish in shoals to the sea-shore seems an intimation that they are intended for human use'; God made domesticated but not wild animals 'conveniently variegated in colour and shape, in order "that mankind may the more readily distinguish and claim their respective property"'; God created fierce animals because they 'provided useful training for war' (Thomas 1983, pp. 18–19).[25] So entrenched did this idea become in Western culture that people were still defending it in the 1830s (Thomas 1983, p. 20; Lovejoy 2009, p. 187). All of this was undergirded by the claim that sapiens, alone in bearing the image of God, possessed an immaterial soul which bestowed the faculty of reason.

Possessing an immaterial soul makes us similar to God. Some theologians today still argue that, since God is an immaterial being who thinks and makes choices, it is natural to think that humans, 'the highest earthly created entities', image God by possessing an immaterial soul that makes us capable of thinking and making choices (Farris 2021, p. 316). But the soul did not just give humans a point of ontological similarity to God; it was also thought to be what made communion with God possible, since reason facilitates contemplation of the divine. Michelle Gonzalez explains:

> For many of the church fathers, the notion of the imago Dei was intimately linked to their understanding of the soul and spirituality. The image was most fully realized in the act of contemplation of God. The human being does not

---

[25] For more, see Thomas (1983, Ch 1) and Turner (1964).

truly realize him or herself unless he or she . . . returns [through contempla-
tion] to the Being in whose image they are created. (Gonzalez 2021, p. 63)

This view also had implications for theological thinking on human psychology. Identifying the uniqueness of humans with the immaterial soul naturally leads to the view that the human ideal involves the immaterial soul
gaining mastery over our animal nature, as here with Augustine: 'That by
which humans are ranked above animals, whatever it is, be it more correctly
called "mind" or "spirit" or both . . . if it dominates and commands the rest of
what a human consists in, then that human being is completely in order'
(Augustine 2010, p. 15). As Eric Meyer (2018) has outlined in a powerful
study, this led Christian scholars to downplay the role our sapien animality
plays in our identity, and to denigrate animality so as to put further distance
between sapiens and other animals.

4.3 The Universe Revealed by Science

Our contemporary view of the world differs markedly from the view just
sketched, in large part due to the scientific revolution, which has been well
described by David Wootton as 'a successful rebellion by the mathematicians
against the authority of the philosophers, and of both against the authority of the
theologians' (Wootton 2015, p. 24). From 1550 onwards, multiple lines of
evidence chipped away at the Aristotelian-Ptolemaic cosmology and Great
Chain of Being metaphysics. After Nicolaus Copernicus dislodged the Earth
from the centre of the universe, Johannes Kepler and Isaac Newton naturalised
the motion of the earthly and heavenly bodies, showing both to be governed by
the same laws. Meanwhile, observations of the planets made with the newly
invented telescope (c. 1608) demonstrated that they were not perfectly uniform
spheres. These developments undermined the idea of a heaven spatially located
just beyond the sphere that bounded the sky. The 'disappearance of the orderly,
layered, cosmos, in which everything had its proper place, and in which the
moral and theological order corresponded with the physical . . . made
a considerable difference to people's conception of their place in the scheme
of things' (Richards 2000, p. 8). Richards explains:

> Spinning around in an infinite universe is decidedly less comfortable than
> being enclosed by spheres and angels and God; and if you disrupt the physics
> of a universe that also incorporates the moral and religious order, you are
> bound to cause some anxiety. Where, if there was no Empyreum, was the
> throne of God? Where was Hell? . . . If the Bible was not literally true in its
> account of heaven and earth, what did that imply for the rest of it? (Richards
> 2000, p. 9)

The large-scale excavations for the canals and railways of the industrial revolution gave scholars access to diverse rock strata across wide geographical areas, which spurred theorising about geological processes and the length of time they needed (Prothero 2017, p. 98) and unveiled an increasing number of fossils. At the start of the nineteenth century, George Cuvier 'showed conclusively that the skeletons of mastodonts and mammoths represented giant animals that could no longer be alive on earth today and must be extinct' (Prothero 2017, p. 134). This and similar discoveries by pioneering fossil hunters such as Mary Anning eventually undermined 'belief in the constancy and permanence of the Creation' (Mayr 2002, p. 5). They also laid the foundation for the work of Charles Darwin on evolution.

Evolution is 'change in the properties of populations of organisms over time' (Mayr 2002, p. 8). Darwin thought there were two things an account of species formation needed to explain: first, the development of new traits within a population (*anagenesis*); second, the splitting of a single breeding population into two species (*cladogenesis*) (Mayr 2002, p. 11). The first of these Darwin explained with his theory of *natural selection*. The second was explained by outlining various ways a breeding population may become isolated, at which point natural selection would eventually lead to divergence. Drawing on Thomas Malthus' idea that populations will tend to increase to use all the available resources, Darwin reasoned that individuals in a given population will soon need to compete for the available resources. On average, those most able to secure the required resources will survive and produce more offspring. Over many generations, populations will acquire traits that allow them to better exploit the resources in their environment. This requires no agency which foresees or plans the traits that come to exist; biological adaptation is a by-product of some individuals being eliminated (Mayr 2002, p. 117ff). Interestingly, once the evidence Darwin and others presented had undermined the general belief in divine design, and so removed the blinkers that that belief had imposed, biologists came to recognise 'the extent to which organisms turned out ... to be riddled with absurdities that no self-respecting designer would have allowed as far as the drawing board' (Richards 2000, p. 1). A nice example of this is the mammalian laryngeal nerve, an evolutionary descendent of the vagus nerve. As 'the ancestors of mammals evolved further and further away from their fish ancestors, nerves and blood vessels found themselves pulled and stretched in puzzling directions, which distorted their spatial relations one to another' (Dawkins 2010, pp. 359–360). In mammals, the laryngeal nerve was forced to take a detour on route to its destination, the larynx. In sapiens this detour amounts to a few inches. In giraffes, the nerve '[o]n its downward journey ... passes within inches of the larynx' only to proceed 'down the whole length of the neck before turning round and going all the way back up again' – a detour of up to 15 feet (Dawkins 2010, p. 360). Not the way one would expect the nerve to have been designed, even if the world were only 'the first rude essay of some infant deity' (Hume 2008, p. 45), much less the creation of the God of Christian theism, but just what one would expect from an unguided process of evolution by natural selection.

Two other features of Darwin's view are worth mentioning. The first is that of common ancestry, according to which 'all the organic beings which have ever lived on this earth have descended from some one primordial form' (Darwin 2008, p. 356). Subsequent findings have corroborated Darwin's claim, and the structure of the evolutionary tree of life is increasingly well-understood. According to current consensus, sapiens first emerged in East Africa around 200,000 years ago, and genetic evidence shows that all humans today derive from a breeding population of no less than 5,000 females (Dunbar 2016, p. 14). Our precursors were *Homo heidelbergensis*, first seen around 500,000 years ago, who themselves emerged from a late subgroup of *Homo erectus* known as *Homo ergaster* (Dunbar 2016, p. 11). Members of *Homo heidelbergensis* developed into *Homo neanderthalensis*, who persisted until around 24,000 years ago. *Homo erectus*, who emerged around 1.8 million years ago and only disappeared 60,000 years ago, possessed the first known worked tool, the Acheulean handaxe, which dates to around 1.7 million years ago (Dunbar 2016, p. 11). *Homo habilis*, a transitional species bridging the genera *Australopithecus* and *Homo*, emerged around 2 million years ago. The ancestors of *Homo habilis* departed from the ancestors of the two extant species of the genus *Pan* – the chimpanzee and the bonobo – around 5–6 million years ago; the ancestors of both diverged from the gorilla lineage 1–2 million years before that (Dunbar 2016, pp. 6–7). The story can be traced back further, of course, but the important point is that the fossil record, comparative anatomy, and genetic evidence (Dunbar 2016, p. 4), all converge on the view that we sapiens are continuous with other animals.

The second point of significance is that the theory of evolution makes claims about all aspects of biological organisms, including their brains and minds. This is significant because of the long history in theology of taking reason to demarcate a qualitative divide between sapiens and other animals. As such, I describe a few select findings on both animal and sapien cognition to give a flavour of what the empirical findings reveal in these areas.

Beginning with animal cognition, consider evidence that animals can form abstractions. The capacity to form judgements about *absolute number* involves understanding that all collections of, say, seven items have something in common, and this requires a capacity for a type of abstraction. Clive Wynne and Monique Udell report that rats, mongoose lemurs, meadow voles, and cowbirds can all discern absolute number to some degree (Wynne and Udell 2021, pp. 85–86). A more advanced numeric skill is the ability to count, which requires further capacities for abstraction. There is some evidence that Nephila spiders have the ability to count to small numbers (King 2021), and similar evidence exists for chimpanzees, macaques, and rhesus monkeys. Fascinatingly, Margaret Livingstone taught macaque monkeys symbols for the numbers 1 through 25 and showed that they could use these symbols to perform addition (Wynne and Udell 2021, p. 93). Another foundation of abstract thought is the ability to understand *same/different concepts*. This involves being able to discern when two stimuli are the same and to generalise this learning to new instances. Studies by one group of scientists have shown that capuchin monkeys, rhesus monkeys, pigeons, Clark's nutcrackers, and black-billed magpies are capable of learning same/different concepts (Wright et al. 2022, pp. 6203–6204). The more advanced capacity for *stimulus equivalence*, again requiring further powers of abstraction, has been found in pigeons, dolphins, sea lions, chimpanzees and beluga whales (Wynne and Udell 2021, pp. 65, 68). Such capacities for abstraction underlie the more advanced learning and problem-solving skills that we see in, for instance, New Caledonian crows and chimpanzees.

In a different vein, primatologist Franz de Waal has presented evidence that several species of social animals have capacities that may be the precursors to the human capacity for empathy (de Waal 2006, p. 24). One example is *emotional contagion*, where 'the emotional state of one individual induces a matching or closely related state in another' (de Waal 2006, p. 26), and for which there is ample evidence among several species of social animal. When sympathy, understood as 'an affective response that consists of feelings of sorrow or concern for a distressed other' (de Waal 2006, p. 26), is added to emotional contagion, we have something approaching empathy. De Waal finds evidence for some measure of empathy in rhesus monkeys, who would 'refuse to pull a chain that delivers food to themselves if doing so shocks a companion' (de Waal 2006, p. 29). When it comes to apes, the evidence for empathy is much stronger. De Waal argues that apes 'have an appreciation of the other's situation and a degree of perspective-taking' which enables them to produce more sophisticated behaviour in response to the distress of others (de Waal 2006, p. 30). In illustrating this, de Waal cites the case of Kuni, a bonobo in Twycross Zoo, who one day captured a starling. Kuni's keeper urged her to let the starling go, and in response Kuni climbed to the top of a tree, carefully unfolded its wings, before throwing the bird into the air (de Waal 2006, p. 31). De Waal explains the significance:

> What Kuni did would obviously have been inappropriate towards a member of her own species. Having seen birds in flight many times, she seemed to

have a notion of what would be good for a bird, thus offering us an anthropoid version of the empathic capacity so enduringly described by Adam Smith as 'changing places in fancy with the sufferer'. (de Waal 2006, p. 31)

De Waal also describes cases of 'altruistic behavior tailored to the specific needs of the other even in novel situations' in apes, instances of consolation and gratitude in chimpanzees, and a sense of fairness evident in capuchin monkeys (de Waal 2006, pp. 33, 42, 45). Marc Bekoff and Jessica Pierce (2009) also provide evidence that some non-humans experience and respond to empathy, while also suggesting that some animals have a sense of justice. And Carl Safina (2020) has detailed the range and depth of emotions experienced by elephants, wolves, and orcas, which include helping and comforting behaviours, and expressions of grief. This shows, contrary to the traditional theological view, that reason and emotion are capacities which can be possessed to a greater or lesser degree, and that reason is not the exclusive possession of us sapiens.

Turning now to the nature of our own mind, two points are worth noting. The first is that multiple lines of evidence point towards a materialist view of the sapien mind. Even before the scientific revolution, some thinkers drew this conclusion based on astute observations of how people think and act under unusual or abnormal circumstances. An example is Julien Offray de La Mettrie, a French physician and philosopher, who was led to a materialist view of the mind by observing how 'hunger, injury, drugs, and sleep affected people's minds' (Hoffmann 2012, p. 24). A materialist view of the mind is supported by a general evolutionary outlook; indeed, evolutionary theory predicts what we observe: our brains have more in common with chimpanzee brains than they do with the brains of dogs, more in common with canine brains than they do with fish brains, and so on. And the similarities are not just anatomical, but genetic. Moreover, contemporary neuroscience is 'rooted in the evolutionary theory that the brain develops in phylogeny by the successive addition of more cephalad parts', such that 'each new addition or enlargement was accompanied by the elaboration of a more complex behavior' (Mountcastle 1982, p. 7). Aspects of our cognition are still rooted in evolutionarily ancient brain systems, even if we have some capacity to regulate the behaviours those older systems give rise to. The point here is not that these advances falsify dualism, but they do undercut many of the reasons given for positing an immaterial soul since, as Nancey Murphy has observed, 'nearly all of the human capacities or faculties once attributed to the soul are now seen to be functions of the brain' (Brown et al. 1998, p. 1).

The second point about sapien cognition relevant to our topic concerns, not the ontology of the mind, but the character of our cognition. This point can be illustrated using findings on the *Wason test*. In this test, subjects are presented with four cards face up, for instance: 'F', 'J', '2', '8'. The subject is told that each card has a letter on one side and a number on the other, and then asked which card or cards must be turned over to determine if the following rule is true: *if a card has an 'F' on one side, then it has a '2' on the other side*. The correct answer for this particular version is 'F' and '8', but most answer 'F' and '2'. The result is significant because to answer correctly requires application of a very simple logical rule. If the traditional theological view of the human person were correct – if we possess a faculty of reason in virtue of which we bear a similarity to God – we might expect extremely good performance on tests like this. As it is, however, only around 10% of people answer correctly – a widely replicated finding.[26] There is no consensus on why most people fail the Wason test. Leda Cosmides and John Tooby (1992) carried out several variations and demonstrated that, if the content *but not the logical structure* of the problem is altered to involve social relationships, then people have no problem giving the correct answer. They think this is evidence that we sapiens evolved a specialised mental capacity for detecting cheats, something we might expect given our highly social nature. More generally, many psychologists believe that much sapien cognition is based on a set of cognitive heuristics and biases: processes which operate quickly and largely without conscious control. Cognitive processes that seem to fall into this category include availability bias, anchoring, myside bias, social proof, the bystander effect, confabulation, and cognitive dissonance, among many others (Sutherland 2011). Hugo Mercier and Dan Sperber think that such phenomena show that we sapiens 'are like other animals: instead of one general inferential ability, [we] use a wide variety of specialized mechanisms' (Mercier and Sperber 2017, p. 6). Such conclusions are contentious, and will no doubt be subject to revision and refinement over the years to come. Still, as Stephen Jay Gould urged, all thinking and curious people should 'support the quest for an evolutionary psychology' (Gould 2001, p. 98). And such a psychology is likely to show that our evolutionary history has affected the structure of our thought and quality of our cognition, which will not only establish a further point of continuity between sapien and non-sapien cognition, but also cast doubt on the traditional theological view of reason.

4.4 The Epistemology of Theology

Perhaps the most straightforward observation to draw from the above sketches is that several beliefs central to the traditional theological outlook – beliefs given vigorous theological defence for hundreds of years – have been falsified

---

[26] For a fuller discussion, see Mercier and Sperber (2017, pp. 39–42).

by scientific findings and quietly abandoned by later generations of theologians: that the earth is around six thousand years old; that the earth is the centre of the universe; that heaven is spatially located; that the moral order of the universe is mirrored in its physical order; that humans derive from a single pair of progenitors; that species boundaries are distinct; that species are static; that extinction is a theological impossibility; that all other creatures were made for sapiens and had some use to us; that there is a qualitative divide between sapiens and all other creatures; that sapiens form an ontological bridge between the terrestrial and celestial realms; that we have no moral obligations to non-human animals; that cognition can only be explained by an immaterial soul; that non-human animals possess no capacity for cognition; that sapiens possess a transcendent rationality that groups us with the angels and God; that humans are incapable of bringing about lasting changes in the natural world; that the actions of the first humans corrupted the entire cosmos – all of these and more have been shown false, or had serious doubt cast on them, by empirical findings.

It may be suggested that these now-abandoned theological beliefs were not part of canonical Christianity, and that therefore their abandonment does little to undermine the central claims of the Christian faith or the epistemology on which it relies. But though true in some cases, things aren't always so simple. For instance, the abandonment of the Aristotelian-Ptolemaic cosmology means that what we believe when we affirm, say, that Christ ascended into heaven, is very different to what those who first affirmed it believed by it. Given that this pertains to the Resurrection, that seems theologically significant. Or consider the belief that extinction was theologically impossible. No one today would defend this claim on theological grounds, yet theologians of previous generations grounded this belief *in the doctrine of God*. Were they mistaken in how they understood God, or in what followed from their understanding of God?

Scientific findings seem to have revealed that the cow and the pig, the dugong and the bonobo, among many others, are sentient creatures worthy of serious ethical consideration. Given that, the fact that, as Mary Midgley put it, for almost 1500 years 'the main official Christian doctrine has simply excluded animals from consideration as not having souls' (1983, p. 11) seems to have implications for the idea that Christian ethics is based on God's own self-revelation. Or again, evolutionary theory puts serious pressure on the idea of an Adamic fall, certainly one which might explain the corruption of the wider cosmos, yet Eden and the Adamic fall are 'the strong central kernel of Christian systematic theology' (Creegan 2013, p. 17). What follows for the epistemology of theology when we face with full seriousness the fact that for over a thousand years theologians placed the now-untenable idea of an Adamic fall at the centre of theology?

As we learn more about non-human animals, and our own animality, there may be additional theological beliefs that become difficult to endorse. And while theologians have done much creative work in revisioning, for instance, the Eden narrative in light of evolution, the implications of this revisioning also need to be fed back into our understanding of divine revelation and the wider epistemological foundations of theology.

4.5 The Image of God

Scientific findings of the sort just surveyed pose a challenge to traditional theological anthropology which posits a qualitative divide between sapiens and all other animals based on the idea that sapiens alone have an immaterial soul. This view entails a discontinuity between sapiens and other animals, but the evidence suggests we sapiens are biologically and psychologically continuous with other creatures. Recognising this does not require us to deny that we humans have the most well-developed cognitive capacities of God's earthly creatures, capacities that allow us, and us alone, to invent language, domesticate crops, live in villages, build cities, create powerful works of art, develop advanced technology, and so on. It does require us to recognise that, as Anna Case-Winters succinctly put it, our place in the world 'is much more modest than we have heretofore imagined' (Case-Winters 2004, p. 816).

Some theologians have responded to this by eschewing the idea that sapiens have an immaterial soul, but retaining the idea that sapiens and only sapiens are made in the image of God. This is usually done by adopting a *functional* account of the image of God. These accounts construe the image of God as a *role* or *function* that we sapiens have been given by God to perform. Functional accounts gained traction among biblical scholars in the 1950s after close textual work on the Old Testament revealed that substantive accounts of the image of God lack a firm scriptural foundation; they have been widely accepted by theologians working on animal or ecological issues.

Andrew Linzey rejects substantive views, noting that 'a good number of [the differences appealed to] have turned out to be not so unique after all' (Linzey 1994, p. 46), and pointing out that some of the proposals for demarcating humans as unique among are 'self-serving, even selfish' (Linzey 1994, p. 46). Linzey thus turns to functional views of the image of God:

> [the functionalist interpretation of the image of God] provides the grounding
> for an ecological and animal-friendly interpretation of the human presence
> in creation. ... [it views] human specialness as consisting ... in exercising
> God-like power over animals – a power that also requires God-like responsi-
> bility. (Linzey 2009b, p. 29)

According to Linzey, the role humans have been given is that of representing God's love to all creation, a task which we should do in a way congruent with God's work on the Cross – by acts of sacrificial service (Linzey 1994, pp. 56–58). Ryan McLaughlin takes a similar approach, saying that being made in the image of God is about making God present in creation (McLaughlin 2014, p. 46), and since we humans 'bear the image of a particular God, the God who is . . .. "for us", even to the point of self-sacrifice', our task as sapiens 'is to act for creation, even to the point of self-sacrifice' (McLaughlin 2014, p. 47).

In addition to the ethical implications, functional accounts of the image of God have consequences for several other areas of theology. One example is Linzey's contention that the force of the injunction to mirror God in acts of self-sacrificial love evaporates unless we endorse the idea, contrary to classical theism, that God suffers. Another, highlighted by Kris Hiuser (2017, p. 193ff), is that, because being made in the image of God is (partly) constitutive of one's identity, the suggestion that we sapiens are to represent God to other animals makes our relationship to those other animals (partly) determinative of who we are.

One objection to thinking that the image of God consists in the role of making God present to other animals concerns whether we are fitting moral subjects for this role. J. M. Coetzee once remarked that we humans are 'the most implacably savage of all beasts' (J. M. Coetzee, blurb to Rowe and McArthur 2021) and there are, alas, good grounds for such a judgement. Evidence suggests that when our ancestors reached Australia around 45,000 years ago, they hunted to extinction twenty-three out of twenty-four species of the native megafauna, including the giant diprotodon, which had lived on the continent for 1.5 million years (Harari 2015, pp. 65–66); within a few hundred years of sapiens reaching New Zealand, most of its megafauna were extinct; as sapiens spread through Eurasia and into North America, the mammoth was driven out, becoming extinct approximately 10,000 years ago; with the arrival of sapiens in North America, the continent lost thirty-four of forty-seven types of large animal, and South America fifty of sixty (Harari 2015, p. 71). Our arrival in a region is also correlated with the disappearance of other human species. And while there is some evidence for minimal interbreeding – for example, initial studies suggest that 1–4 percent of the DNA of populations in the Middle East and Europe is Neanderthal[27] – it seems that the major factors behind their disappearance were being outcompeted and sometimes exterminated by sapiens. Around 11,000 years ago, sapiens began subjugating other species in order to make them easier to use and abuse for our own purposes (something we like to call

---

[27] This reinforces the point about the blurred lines of species boundaries, since it suggests sapiens and neandertals were "not completely separate species . . . nor just different populations of the same species" Harari (2015, p. 16).

'domestication'). This proceeds apace today with technological tools such as genetic engineering and economic tools such as market fundamentalism, pursued in their most extreme forms by nations with a deep Christian heritage. We also have a long history of tormenting animals for entertainment. Traditional Christian theology played a role in making possible some of the more systematic types of exploitation, since it enabled people to see themselves as distinct from the natural world in a way which licensed the latter's exploitation (see Paul Tyson (2021) for a discussion of this with respect to climate change).

These observations do not falsify the claim that we sapiens have a special calling to represent God to other creatures, but our track record is somewhat discordant with the idea. It is perhaps akin to suggesting that someone who has subjected their partner to years of gaslighting, mental torment, and physical abuse, has been chosen by God as the one who has the special task of telling the abused about God's love. One might suspect that were a Japanese sea lion or Bubal hartebeest,[28] not to mention a pig or chicken, informed that we sapiens are God's special co-redeemers, here to lead them into divine presence, they would ask to be excused of any such 'redemption'. Adopting a broader, critical perspective to the Christian tradition might well lead to the conclusion that the appeal to functional accounts of the image of God here is, to appropriate words of John Hick, 'one of those theological epicycles by which it is sought to abandon an untenable traditional idea whilst at the same time retaining the traditional language' (Hick 1993, p. 129).

An alternative response to the demise of substantive views of the image of God is to shift focus away from the image of God. David Cunningham notes that 'the primary focus of God's relational life *ad extra*' is not humanity but all flesh (Cunningham 2009, p. 114). This observation helps displace the binary distinction between sapiens and all other creatures, and enables us to attend to the 'rather fluid boundaries' between creatures revealed by the sciences. Cunningham also notes that the idea of a hard-and-fast demarcation should always have been thought problematic, since any entity can image another to a greater or lesser degree, and it is possible to image things in a variety of ways (Cunningham 2009, pp. 110–111). This gives theological warrant for saying that all created objects image God in some way (Cunningham 2009, p. 112). Still, rather than pursuing this line of thought, Cunningham suggests that theology should focus on the idea that God became flesh. Such a focus will 'reshape the doctrine of creation' (Cunningham 2009, p. 114). It would also lay the foundation for a view of the Incarnation that prioritises God's becoming flesh over God's becoming human (Cunningham 2009, p. 116), which would in

---

[28] Two of the many species we've hunted to extinction in the recent past.

turn lead to the view that all creation needs to be redeemed (Cunningham 2009, pp. 116–117).

There are, of course, other theological responses to the undermining of the traditional substantive view of the image of God. What should be clear, though, is that it is no small task to rethink theology in light of this, and the revisions required may well be significant.

4.6 The Incarnation

In Christian thought, the 'concept of incarnation is intrinsically related to its soteriological purpose' (Gregersen 2015, p. 11), and the dominant views of both have construed them as applicable only to humans. Why did God the Son become incarnate in Jesus of Nazareth? Why did God resurrect Jesus from the dead? The Chalcedonian Definition of 451 answers that the Son of God, 'for us and our salvation came down from the heavens, and was incarnate of the Holy Spirit and the Virgin Mary, and lived as man'. This suggests that it was for humans alone that God became a man: humans sinned, and God became human to save humans from their sin – a point agreed on by Anselm, Aquinas, Bonaventure, Luther, and Calvin (Edwards 2019, p. 8).

David Clough points out that this position depends on two problematic assumptions. The first is that sapiens are the only creatures capable of sinning. The second is that creatures who are incapable of sinning need no reconciliation. Rejecting either one of these assumptions motivates the search for accounts of the Incarnation and Atonement that encompass more than just sapiens. In assessing the first claim it is useful to introduce a distinction between redemption (or rescue) and reconciliation. I draw here from Clough (2012, p. 120), but I do not claim this is how Clough understands the distinction. I will say that a creature needs *redemption* or *rescue* when that creature suffers but cannot extricate themselves from the suffering. In this sense, nothing is implied about whether one has done something wrong or sinned, nor even about whether one has the capacity to do wrong. By contrast, a creature needs *reconciliation* if they have done something wrong which has alienated them from another individual. Whether reconciliation implies one has sinned depends on whether one connects sin with responsibility, a topic to which I return below.

Clough gives two reasons in defence of the idea that some non-sapiens sin. First, several biblical passages state or imply that animals can sin. For example, Genesis 6 says that 'all living creatures shared in the corruption that provoked God's wrath' (Clough 2012, p. 108), while Genesis 3, Genesis 9, Exodus 19, Leviticus 15–16, and Hebrews 12 depict animals as the subjects of wrongdoing or describe actions for which both humans and other animals will be punished (and punishment implies sin) (Clough 2012, p. 109). Clough also notes the long tradition in Europe of 'holding non-human animals responsible under the law': animals such as locusts, snakes, mice, pigs, bulls, eels and more were charged and tried in the courts, if not frequently, then at least regularly from around 800 to 1900 (Clough 2012, pp. 109–110). This practice was justified with appeal to Exodus 21, which leads Clough to conclude that 'we need to reckon with [a] . . . tradition in which the Bible was interpreted to indicate that non-human animals were capable of wrongdoing, even to the point of the considerable expense of putting them on trial' (Clough 2012, p. 112).

Neither reason is convincing. Suppose we agree that the correct interpretation of a given biblical passage implies that a non-human animal bears responsibility, and so sinned. All other things equal, this seems to provide more reason for rejecting the veracity of the passage in question than it does for concluding that some non-humans can sin. Moreover, it's not clear we could follow through with Clough's suggestion consistently. All but one of the passages Clough cites are from the Pentateuch and Joshua. If we take them at face value, and conclude animals can sin, should we also think that violating the Sabbath, cursing God, and being a 'wayward son' are sins serious enough to deserve the death penalty? Or again: Clough seems to float the idea that the snake who tempts Eve in Genesis 3 could have been a real snake, which would mean this passage is evidence that snakes can sin (Clough 2012, p. 108). But does that mean Genesis 3 also provides evidence that snakes can talk? It would seem so, given that the snake's sin requires talking. But this would be a *reductio* of the approach. Clough's appeal to the legal tradition does nothing to bolster the case. Do we really think, for instance, that the fact that in 1474 magistrates in Basle sentenced a cock to be burned at the stake for laying an egg – a heinous crime, since cocks' eggs could be hatched into cockatrices that sorcerers could use to kill people – as evidence that the medievals had correctly interpreted Exodus 21 (Evans 1997, pp. 162–163)? More reasonable, I think, is that such historical episodes are evidence of an easily 'excited imagination tainted with superstition' (Evans 1997, p. 162).

Clough's second reason concerns evidence from ethology, and here the ground is firmer. Given that sapiens are continuous with other animals, we should expect that some animals will possess by degrees some of the capacities that comprise our ability for moral thought and action – and indeed, we've already seen evidence for this in the discussion of de Waal's work above. Clough makes the case that some non-sapiens sin by discussing a behaviour observed among chimpanzees by Jane Goodall and her team:

> In 1975 . . . Tanzanian field staff observed an adult female, who had been
> named Passion, take an infant from a mother, Gilka, kill the infant by biting

its forehead and consume its body, with Passion's daughter Pom. (Clough 2012, p. 112)

The same thing happened the following year with Gilka's next baby, and on two other occasions with another female and two of her babies. Most interesting is Goodall's report of the reaction of several other chimpanzees unrelated to Passion and Pom: 'Sparrow . . . came alone, picked up a bit of meat, after staring and staring, sniffed it, flung it down and vigorously wiped her fingers on the tree trunk. Her daughter, Sandi, did exactly the same' (Goodall, as cited in Clough 2012, p. 113).

Should we construe the actions of Passion and Pom as sinful? There are several notions of sin that may apply to the actions of Passion and Pom. As Clough sees it, '[t]he Augustinian characterization of sin as distorted desire and the feminist image of sin as the breakdown of right relationships are both clearly apt representations of the chimpanzee infanticides' (2012, p. 116). However, much care is needed here. There is no doubt that we can articulate an account of sin as distorted desire, and label as sinful the harmful actions which flow from such desires. Such accounts of sin give us a way to articulate something of the tragedy of human life because, as Clough (2012, p. 117) notes, before we sapiens are able to exercise any freedom at all, we have already become tangled up in structures that produce injustices. To recognise the usefulness of such broad concepts of sin, however, is a long way from having established that these accounts of sin *entail that the person is thereby responsible for the action performed.* Moreover, we have good reason for thinking such accounts of sin cannot entail responsibility, namely, that they disconnect sin from choice, freedom, and agency. To illustrate the problem: one may have a disordered desire, through no fault of one's own, as a result of suffering severe abuse, and one may be alienated from that desire, wanting and seeking to be rid of it, yet that desire may still cause one to act in ways that are harmful to others. It would be unjust to hold someone responsible for such a desire or its resultant action – things over which the person has no control. And we should therefore avoid connecting this notion of sin to responsibility.[29]

To maintain that sin entails responsibility, we need to connect sin to deliberate choice and intentional wrongdoing. Might the actions of Passion and Pom count as sinful on this construal? Clough suggests that unless we hold that non-human animals are automata, we cannot 'avoid the conclusion that the actions of the chimpanzees were some combination of free and forced choices', and therefore to some degree sinful (Clough 2012, p. 113). I think this conclusion is correct, though the reasoning too quick. A case can be made for thinking that

---

[29] See Kittle (2024) for more argument to this effect.

moral responsibility requires recognising that the action under a given description is wrong. Clough argues against this requirement on the grounds that:

> it fails to reflect the complexity of the relationship between the concepts of sin, guilt and responsibility in the Christian tradition. At the root of the doctrine of original sin is the recognition that we do not begin life with a clean slate and then make a series of deliberate choices that result in our being awarded good or bad marks. (Clough 2012, p. 117)

But this is mistaken. It is possible to hold that any concept of sin-as-entailing-responsibility should be connected with the making of deliberate well-informed choices while also holding that there is another, broader concept of sin that plays the role Clough outlines here. These two notions have been assimilated in some theological systems, but they need not be run together. So, the question is: given the choice-based notion of sin, do Passion and Pom bear some degree of responsibility? Tentatively, we can answer 'yes, maybe'. We can answer this way because we have evidence of highly-developed faculties possessed by chimpanzees. But this same evidence requires a significant caveat: the capacities of chimpanzees exceed those of most other species, but fall far short of the capacities sapiens possess. That must be borne in mind when considering the type or degree of responsibility for which chimpanzees may be apt candidates. If we tentatively conclude chimpanzees may be able to perform morally wrong actions, we should also add that they can bear nothing like the sort of responsibility human adults can bear. Their capacity for moral thought and action may be similar to that of a very small child, or a form of proto-morality. This is theologically interesting, but it places severe constraints on the theological use to which the affirmation that some non-sapiens can sin can be put.

If some non-humans can sin, even in small measure, can they be reconciled to God? Clough answers yes, and proposes extending the scope of the Son's incarnation as Jesus to cover all creatures. Clough finds much in the New Testament that envisages the Incarnation as a cosmic event: 'the fundamental New Testament assertion concerning the incarnation, . . . is not that God became a member of the species *Homo sapiens*, but that God took on flesh, the stuff of living creatures' (Clough 2012, p. 84). Therefore:

> if we judge it illegitimate to discriminate between Jews and Gentiles or women and men on the basis of the kind of creature in whom God became incarnate, it seems that we should also consider it illegitimate to discriminate between humans and other animals. (Clough 2012, p. 84)

To expand the scope of the Incarnation to non-humans, there are perhaps two main ways forward: reconstrue the Incarnation as primarily about God's taking on animality, or flesh; or, explore the possibility of multiple incarnations.

Clough prefers the first option. He thinks that the creeds of Nicaea, Constantinople and Chalcedon – framed as they are in terms of God taking on human nature – are apt to mislead,[30] but he also maintains that they are nevertheless accurate, and holds that expanding the scope of the Incarnation to 'the stuff of living creatures' is an augmentation of the creedal position (Clough 2012, p. 84).

Still, Clough's position is at odds with some ways of understanding the Atonement. For instance, on some accounts it is essential to the Atonement that '*humanity* is taken into God for ever' (Hebblethwaite 2004, p. 66). One motivation for this view is the idea that God takes on human nature precisely because God's act of reconciliation requires God to do something qua human: e.g., to perfectly fulfil the law as a human. Another is that God the Son assumes a human nature because only that which is assumed is healed and thereby reconciled. Clough's approach seems to be incompatible with these types of Atonement account. A similar thing may be true, although for very different reasons, for moral influence accounts of the Atonement. On such accounts, Jesus overcomes sin by providing a moral exemplar which shows people the depth of their sin, leading them to repentance. But, as Hiuser points out, it is doubtful such a view could be extended to non-human animals, for non-humans cannot comprehend the accounts of Jesus' life and work (Hiuser 2017, p. 17).

In contrast to those who would expand the scope of the Incarnation, some have explored the possibility of multiple incarnations. Blake Hereth (2019) has presented two arguments for this. The first is the *power argument* which says, very roughly, that if God is a member of group *G* but not a member of group *S*, then members of group *G* have decisive power over members of group *S*. That, according to Hereth, is unfair, and so reason to think God would avoid that situation by becoming a member of both groups (Hereth 2019, pp. 187–189). The second is the *solidarity argument* which depends on the claim that one reason for God's becoming incarnate is to show solidarity with oppressed groups. If we accept that claim, then we have reason to think that God will become incarnate as a member of any species which suffers unduly; to do less is to 'identify with creaturely oppression only minimally' (Hereth 2019, p. 197). In short, non-human animals 'are oppressed in ways most humans are not, and God displays a lack of solidarity with them unless God suffers as they suffer' (Hereth 2019, p. 197).

Both of Hereth's arguments suggest that God will become incarnate as a member of all oppressed groups. But how should we draw group boundaries?

---

[30] This is a striking concession, given the role these creeds play in the formation of doctrine and practice.

We've already seen that 'evolutionary biology makes clear that species bound-aries are surprisingly hard to define' (Clough 2012, p. 82). Would God's becoming incarnate as a member of *Homo sapiens* suffice to show solidarity with *Homo heidelbergensis*? And what about the individuals intermediate between those two species? Hereth is explicit that the power argument 'supports not only the inclusion of non-human animals within the Godhead, but also disabled individuals, people of color, queer individuals, women, etc.' (Hereth 2019, p. 192). According to Dustin Crummett, this implies there will be 'a vast number' of human incarnations, something that he thinks is 'in tension with traditional Christianity' (Crummett 2021, p. 143). The solidarity argument may imply even more. If God doesn't display solidarity 'unless God suffers as they suffer', then we will certainly need incarnate 'saviors for every particular oppressed group' (Crummett 2021, p. 148), but may also need to hold that God becomes incarnate as every oppressed person, since the suffering of each oppressed person is unique. If nothing else, this latter idea seems empirically false. But it also embodies a point that has resurfaced throughout this work, namely, that attempting to take animals seriously as religious subjects can lead to some revisionary theological proposals. In any case, Hereth's position is, to use Crummett's words, 'bold and innovative', and even if ultimately found unworkable, their work is a valuable exploration of the Incarnation which takes animal subjects seriously.

4.7 Summary

Gary Steiner has suggested that, because the Christian tradition overwhelming tends away from treating animals with compassion, to generate an animal-friendly Christian ethic we may have to 'loosen the standards for our own interpretation of Scripture' to enable 'radically revisionist readings' (Steiner 2010, p. 114). Something similar may turn out to be true of theology more generally: the degree to which Christianity can generate an animal-friendly theology will depend in part on how much revisionism we allow. And while revisionary theologies are possible, the historical character of Christianity means that this should, at the very least, leave us a little unsettled. As Susan Frank Parsons has written, 'Coming to terms with our inheritance is not always a comfortable thing, for we are apt to discover both how profoundly we are bound to, and yet how considerably we disagree with, those who bequeath an intellectual and spiritual life to us' (Parsons 2004, p. 114).

References

Adams, C. J., 2010. *The Sexual Politics of Meat*. New York: Continuum.

Adams, C. J., 2012. What about Dominion in Genesis? In T. York and A. Alexis-Baker, eds. *A Faith Embracing All Creatures*. Eugene, OR: Cascade Books, pp. 1–12.

Adams, M. M., 1999. *Horrendous Evils and the Goodness of God*. Ithaca, NY: Cornell University Press.

Aquinas, S.T., 1947. *Summa Theologica*. New York: Benziger Bros.

Attenborough, D., 1990. *The Trials of Life*. Boston: Little Brown.

Augustine, 2010. *On the Free Choice of the Will*. Cambridge: Cambridge University Press.

Banner, M. C., 1999. *Christian Ethics and Contemporary Moral Problems*. Cambridge: Cambridge University Press.

Bauckham, R., 2011. *Living with Other Creatures*. Waco, TX: Baylor University Press.

Bekoff, M., and Pierce, J., 2009. *Wild Justice*. Chicago: University of Chicago Press.

Berkman, J., 2014. From Theological Speciesism to a Theological Ethology. *Journal of Moral Theology*, 3 (2), pp. 11–34.

Brown, W. S., Murphy, N. C., and Malony, H. N., eds., 1998. *Whatever Happened to the Soul?* Minneapolis: Fortress Press.

Calder, T., 2007. Is the Privation Theory of Evil Dead? *American Philosophical Quarterly*, 44 (4), pp. 371–381.

Case-Winters, A., 2004. Rethinking the Image of God. *Zygon*, 39 (4), pp. 813–826.

Chisholm, R. M., 1990. The Defeat of Good and Evil. In M. M. Adams and R. M. Adams, eds. *The Problem of Evil*. Oxford: Oxford University Press, pp. 53–68.

Clough, D. L., 2012. *On Animals: Volume 1 – Systematic Theology*. London: T & T Clark International.

Clough, D. L., 2019. *On Animals: Volume 2 – Theological Ethics*. London: Bloomsbury.

Cortez, M., 2010. *Theological Anthropology*. London: T & T Clark International.

Cosmides, L., and Tooby, J., 1992. Cognitive Adaptations for Social Exchange. In J. H. Barkow, L. Cosmides, and J. Tooby, eds. *The Adapted Mind*. New York: Oxford University Press, pp. 163–228.

Coulon, M., Deputte, B. L., Heyman, Y., Baudoin, C., 2009. Individual Recognition in Domestic Cattle (Bos taurus): Evidence from 2D-Images of Heads from Different Breeds. *PloS one*, 4 (2), e4441.

Creegan, N. H., 2013. *Animal Suffering and the Problem of Evil*. New York: Oxford University Press.

Crummett, D., 2021. Taming Zootheism. *Journal of Analytic Theology*, 9, pp. 137–157.

Crummett, D., 2022. Human Dominion and Wild Animal Suffering. *Religious Studies*, 58 (4), pp. 814–830.

Cunningham, D. S., 2008. *Christian Ethics. The End of The Law*. London: Routledge.

Cunningham, D. S., 2009. The Way of All Flesh. In C. Deane-Drummond and D. Clough, eds. *Creaturely Theology*. London: SCM Press, pp. 100–117.

Darwin, C., 2008. *On the Origin of Species*. New York: Oxford University Press.

Dawkins, S., 2010. *The Greatest Show on Earth*. New York: Free Press.

de Waal, F., 2006. *Primates and Philosophers*. Princeton: Princeton University Press.

Derrida, J., 2002. The Animal That Therefore I Am (More to Follow). *Critical Inquiry*, 29 (2), pp. 369–418.

Donovan, J., and Adams, C. J., 2007. Introduction. In J. Donovan and C. J. Adams, eds. *The Feminist Care Tradition in Animal Ethics. A Reader*. New York: Columbia University Press, pp. 1–20.

Dougherty, T. A., 2014. *The Problem of Animal Pain*. Basingstoke: Palgrave Macmillian.

Dunbar, R. I. M., 2016. *Human Evolution*. New York: Oxford University Press.

Edwards, D., 2019. *Deep Incarnation*. Maryknoll: Orbis Books.

Esvelt, K., 2019. *When Are We Obligated To Edit Wild Creatures?* [online]. Upworthy Science. https://upworthyscience.com/when-are-we-obligated-to-edit-wild-creatures/particle-3 [Accessed 26 October 2024].

Evans, E. P., 1997. *The Criminal Prosecution and Capital Punishment of Animals*. London: Faber and Faber.

Farains, E. J., 2011. Theology and Animals. In L. Kemmerer, ed. *Sister Species. Women, Animals and Social Justice*. Chicago: University of Illinois Press, pp. 102–109.

Farris, J. R., 2021. The Soul as Imago Dei: Modernizing Traditional Theological Anthropology. In J. Arcadi and J. T. Turner, eds. *The T&T Clark Handbook of Analytic Theology*. London: T&T Clark, pp. 311–324.

Foer, J. S., 2009. *Eating Animals*. New York: Little Brown and Company.

Gilhus, I. S., 2006. *Animals, Gods, and Humans*. London: Routledge.

Gill, R., ed., 2012. *The Cambridge Companion to Christian Ethics*. Cambridge: Cambridge University Press.

Gonzalez, M. A., 2021. Created for God and for Each Other: Our Imago Dei. In M. A. Hinsdale and S. Okey, eds. *T&T Clark Handbook of Theological Anthropology*. London: Bloomsbury Academic, pp. 61–70.

Gooder, P., 2011. *Heaven*. Eugene, OR: Cascade Books.

Gould, S. J., 2001. More Things in Heaven and Earth. In H. Rose and S. P. R. Rose, eds. *Alas, Poor Darwin*. London: Vintage.

Gregersen, N. H., 2015. Introduction. In N. H. Gregersen, ed. *Incarnation*. Minneapolis: Fortress Press, pp. 1–21.

Gruen, L., 2007. Empathy and Vegetarian Commitments. In J. Donovan and C. J. Adams, eds. *The Feminist Care Tradition in Animal Ethics. A Reader*. New York: Columbia University Press, pp. 333–343.

Grumett, D., and Muers, R., 2010. *Theology on the Menu*. London: Routledge.

Harari, Y. N., 2015. *Sapiens. A Brief History of Humankind*. New York: Harper.

Harnack, A. von, 1898. *History of Dogma: Vol 5*. London: Williams and Norgate.

Hauerwas, S., and Wells, S., 2011. *The Blackwell Companion to Christian Ethics*. 2nd ed. Chichester: Wiley-Blackwell.

Hebblethwaite, B., 2004. *Philosophical Theology and Christian Doctrine*. Oxford: Wiley-Blackwell.

Hereth, B., 2019. Animal Gods. In B. Hereth and K. Timpe, eds. *The Lost Sheep in Philosophy of Religion*. New York: Taylor & Francis, pp. 183–207.

Hick, J., 1993. *The Metaphor of God Incarnate*. Louisville: John Knox Press.

Hiuser, K., 2017. *Animals, Theology and The Incarnation*. London: SCM Press.

Hobgood-Oster, L., 2010. *The Friends We Keep*. London: Darton, Longman and Todd.

Hoffmann, P. M., 2012. *Life's Ratchet*. New York: Basic Books.

Hume, C. W., 1956. *The Status of Animals in the Christian Religion*. London: The Universities Federation for Animal Welfare.

Hume, D., 2008. *Dialogues Concerning Natural Religion*. Oxford: Oxford University Press.

Jenson, R. W., 1999. *Systematic Theology. Volume 2*. New York: Oxford University Press.

Joy, M., 2011. *Why We Love Dogs, Eat Pigs and Wear Cows*. San Francisco: Conari Press.

Kemmerer, L., 2012. *Animals and World Religions*. New York: Oxford University Press.

King, B. J., 2021. *Animals' Best Friends*. Chicago: University of Chicago Press.

Kingston, A. R., 1967. Theodicy and Animal Welfare. *Theology*, 70 (569), pp. 482–488.

Kittle, S., 2022. God Is (Probably) a Cause among Causes. *Theology and Science*, 20 (2), pp. 247–262.

Kittle, S., 2024. Science, Determinism, and Free Will. In M. Harris, ed. *God and the Book of Nature*. Abingdon: Routledge, pp. 193–213.

Kojonen, R., 2024. Why Evolution Does Not Make the Problem of Evil Worse. *Faith and Philosophy*, 39 (3), pp. 388–406.

Lactantius, 1965. *The Minor Works*. New York: The Catholic University of America Press.

Lakoff, G., 2014. *The All-New Don't Think of an Elephant!* White River Junction: Chelsea Green.

Le Guin, U. K., 2002. *The Dispossessed*. London: HarperCollins.

Lewis, C. S., 1940. *The Problem of Pain*. London: HarperCollins.

Linzey, A., 1976. *Animal Rights. A Christian Perspective*. London: SCM Press.

Linzey, A., 1987. *Christianity and the Rights of Animals*. London: SPCK.

Linzey, A., 1994. *Animal Theology*. London: SCM Press.

Linzey, A., 1998. *Animal Gospel. Christian Faith as Though Animals Mattered*. London: Hodder & Stoughton.

Linzey, A., 2001. Vegetarianism as a Biblical Ideal. In K. S. Walters and L. Portmess, eds. *Religious Vegetarianism*. Albany: State University of New York Press, pp. 126–139.

Linzey, A., 2009a. *Creatures of the Same God*. New York: Lantern Books.

Linzey, A., 2009b. *Why Animal Suffering Matters*. Oxford: Oxford University Press.

Linzey, C., 2022. *Developing Animal Theology*. London: Routledge Taylor & Francis Group.

Lloyd, M., 1998. Are Animals Fallen? In A. Linzey and D. Yamamoto, eds. *Animals on the Agenda*. London: SCM, pp. 147–160.

Long, D. S., and Miles, R., eds., 2023. *The Routledge Companion to Christian Ethics*. Abingdon: Routledge.

Lovejoy, A. O., 2009. *The Great Chain of Being*. London: Transaction Publishers.

Mance, H., 2021. *How to Love Animals*. New York: Viking.

Marino, L., 2022. Bovine Cognition. In J. Vonk and T. K. Shackelford, eds. *Encyclopedia of Animal Cognition and Behavior*. Cham: Springer, pp. 858–863.

Martin, R., and Barresi, J., 2006. *The Rise and Fall of Soul and Self*. New York: Columbia University Press.

Mathewes, C. T., 2010. *Understanding Religious Ethics*. Oxford: Blackwell.

Mayr, E., 2002. *What Evolution Is*. London: Weidenfeld & Nicolson.

McDaniel, J. B., 1989. *Of God and Pelicans*. Louisville: John Knox Press.

McDannell, C., and Lang, B., 1990. *Heaven. A History*. New York: Vintage Books.

McLaughlin, R. P., 2014. *Christian Theology and the Status of Animals*. Basingstoke: Palgrave Macmillan.

McLaughlin, R. P., 2019. How Good is Nature? In A. Linzey, ed. *The Routledge Handbook of Religion and Animal Ethics*. London: Routledge and Taylor & Francis Group, pp. 327–336.

McLaughlin, R. P., 2023. Nonhuman Animals in Christian Theology. *St Andrews Encyclopaedia of Theology*. www.saet.ac.uk/Christianity/NonhumanAnimalsinChristianTheology.

Mercier, H., and Sperber, D., 2017. *The Enigma of Reason*. Cambridge, MA: Harvard University Press.

Messer, N., 2009. Natural Evil After Darwin. In M. S. Northcott and R. J. Berry, eds. *Theology after Darwin*. London: Paternoster Publications, pp. 139–154.

Messer, N., 2019. Evolution, Animal Suffering, and Ethics. In A. Linzey, ed. *The Routledge Handbook of Religion and Animal Ethics*. London: Routledge and Taylor & Francis Group, pp. 337–346.

Messer, N., 2020. *Science in Theology*. London: T&T Clark.

Meyer, E. D., 2018. *Inner Animalities*. New York: Fordham University Press.

Midgley, M., 1983. *Animals and Why They Matter*. Harmondsworth: Penguin Books.

Miller, D. K., 2010. *'And who is my neighbor?': Reading animal ethics through the lens of the Good Samaritan*. PhD thesis, The University of Edinburgh.

Mountcastle, V. B., 1982. *The Mindful Brain*. Cambridge, MA: The MIT press.

Murdock, G. K., 2022. Artiodactyl Cognition. In J. Vonk and T. K. Shackelford, eds. *Encyclopedia of Animal Cognition and Behavior*. Cham: Springer, pp. 446–452.

Murray, M. J., 2008. *Nature Red in Tooth and Claw*. Oxford: Oxford University Press.

Neiman, S., 2002. *Evil in Modern Thought: An Alternative History of Philosophy*. Princeton: Princeton University Press.

Nullens, P., and Michener, R. T., 2013. *The Matrix of Christian Ethics*. Downers Grove: IVP.

Parsons, S. F., 2004. Feminist Theology as Dogmatic Theology. In S. F. Parsons, ed. *The Cambridge Companion to Feminist Theology*. Cambridge: Cambridge University Press, pp. 114–132.

Peacocke, A. R., 1993. *Theology for a Scientific Age*. Minneapolis: Fortress Press.

Plantinga, A., 1974. *God, Freedom and Evil*. Grand Rapids: William B. Eerdmans.

Polkinghorne, J. C., 1991. *Reason and Reality*. London: S.P.C.K.

Pouca, C. V., Tosetto, L., and Brown, C., 2021. A Fish Memory Tale. In A. B. Kaufman, J. Call, and J. C. Kaufman, eds. *The Cambridge Handbook of Animal Cognition*. Cambridge: Cambridge University Press, pp. 140–173.

Prothero, D. R., 2017. *Evolution*. New York: Columbia University Press.

Prummer, D. M., 1957. *Handbook of Moral Theology*. New York: P. J. Kenedy & Sons.

Rachels, J., 1990. *Created from Animals*. Oxford: Oxford University Press.

Ray, J., 1693. *Three Physico-Theological Discourses*. 2nd ed. London: Sam Smith.

Ricard, M., 2016. *A Plea for the Animals*. Boulder: Shambhala.

Richards, J. R., 2000. *Human Nature After Darwin*. London: Routledge.

Rickaby, J., 1901. *Moral Philosophy*. London: Longmans, Green.

Robertson, R., 2020. *The Enlightenment. The Pursuit of Happiness, 1680–1790*. London: Allen Lane.

Rolston, H., 1994. Does Nature Need to Be Redeemed? *Zygon*, 29 (2), pp. 205–229.

Rolston, H., 2018. Redeeming a Cruciform Nature. *Zygon*, 53 (3), pp. 739–751.

Rowe, M., and McArthur, J.-A., 2021. *The Animals Are Leaving Us*. Brooklyn: Lantern & Media.

Ryder, R. D., 1989. *Animal Revolution. Changing Attitudes towards Speciesism*. Oxford: Basil Blackwell.

Safina, C., 2020. *Beyond Words*. London: Souvenir Press.

Schneider, J., 2021a. *Animal Suffering and the Darwinian Problem of Evil*. Cambridge: Cambridge University Press.

Schneider, J., 2021b. *Animal Suffering and the Darwinian Problem of Evil: A Rejoinder* [online]. Carl F. H. Henry Center for Theological Understanding. https://henrycenter.tiu.edu/2021/04/animal-suffering-and-the-darwinian-problem-of-evil-a-rejoinder/ [Accessed 20 September 2024].

Singer, P., 2002. *Animal Liberation*. 2nd ed. New York: Ecco.

Slootweg, P., 2021. *Teeth and Talons Whetted for Slaughter. Divine Attributes and Suffering Animals in Historical Perspective (1600–1961)*. Amsterdam: Vrije Universiteit.

Sollereder, B. N., 2019. *God, Evolution, and Animal Suffering*. London: Routledge.

Southgate, C., 2008a. Protological and Eschatological Vegetarianism. In D. Grumett and R. Muers, eds. *Eating and Believing*. London: T & T Clark, pp. 247–265.

Southgate, C., 2008b. *The Groaning of Creation*. Louisville: Westminster John Knox Press.

Southgate, C., 2011. Re-reading Genesis, John, and Job. *Zygon*, 46 (2), pp. 370–395.

Southgate, C., 2014. Divine Glory in a Darwinian World. *Zygon*, 49 (4), pp. 784–807.

Southgate, C., 2017. Cosmic Evolution and Evil. In C. V. Meister and P. K. Moser, eds. *The Cambridge Companion to the Problem of Evil*. New York: Cambridge University Press, pp. 147–165.

Southgate, C., 2018. 'Free-Process' and 'Only Way' Arguments. In S. P. Rosenberg, ed. *Finding Ourselves After Darwin: Conversations on the Image of God, Original Sin, and the Problem of Evil*. Grand Rapids, MI: Baker Academic, pp. 293–307.

Southgate, C., 2023. *Monotheism and the Suffering of Animals in Nature*. Cambridge: Cambridge University Press.

Steiner, G., 2010. *Anthropocentrism and Its Discontents*. Pittsburgh: University of Pittsburgh Press.

Stump, E., 2022. *The Image of God*. Oxford: Oxford University Press.

Sutherland, N. S., 2011. *Irrationality*. London: Pinter & Martin.

Thomas, K., 1983. *Man and the Natural World*. New York: Pantheon Books.

Torgerson-White, L., 2022. Animal Emotion in Farmed Animal Welfare Assessment. In J. Vonk and T. K. Shackelford, eds. *Encyclopedia of Animal Cognition and Behavior*. Cham: Springer, pp. 272–277.

Torrance, T. F., 1981. *Divine and Contingent Order*. Oxford: Oxford University Press.

Turner, E. S., 1964. *All Heaven in a Rage*. London: Michael Joseph.

Tyson, P. G., 2021. *Theology and Climate Change*. London: Routledge.

van Helden, A., 1985. *Measuring the Universe*. Chicago: University of Chicago Press.

Waddell, H., and Gibbings, R., 1995. *Beasts and Saints*. London: Darton, Longman and Todd.

Ward, A., 2022. *The Social Lives of Animals*. London: Profile Books.

Webb, S. H., 1998. *On God and Dogs*. New York: Oxford University Press.

Wells, S., Quash, B., and Eklund, R. A., 2017. *Introducing Christian Ethics*. Hoboken: John Wiley & Sons.

Wennberg, R. N., 2003. *God, Humans, and Animals. An Invitation to Enlarge Our Moral Universe*. Grand Rapids, MI: William B. Eerdmans.

Westberg, D., 2015. *Renewing Moral Theology*. Downers Grove, IL: IVP Academic.

Wildman, W., 2008a. Ground-of-Being Theologies. In P. Clayton and Z. Simpson, eds. *The Oxford Handbook of Religion and Science*. Oxford: Oxford University Press, pp. 613–632.

Wildman, W., 2008b. Incongruous Goodness, Perilous Beauty, Disconcerting Truth. In N. C. Murphy, R. J. Russell, and W. R. Stoeger, eds. *Physics and Cosmology*. Cambridge: University of Notre Dame Press, pp. 267–294.

Williams, N. P., 1924. *The Ideas of the Fall and Original Sin*. London: Longmans, Green.

Williams, P. A., 2001. *Doing without Adam and Eve*. Minneapolis: Fortress Press.

Wirzba, N., 2011. *Food and Faith*. New York: Cambridge University Press.

Wogaman, J. P., 2011. *Christian Ethics*. 2nd ed. Louisville: Westminster John Knox Press.

Wootton, D., 2015. *The Invention of Science*. London: Allen Lane.

Wright, A. A., Katz, J. S., and Kelly, D. M., 2022. Same/Different Learning. In J. Vonk and T. K. Shackelford, eds. *Encyclopedia of Animal Cognition and Behavior*. Cham: Springer, pp. 6200–6210.

Wynne, C. D. L., and Udell, M. A. R., 2021. *Animal Cognition*. 3rd ed. London: Bloomsbury Academic.

Young, R. A., 2012. *Is God a Vegetarian?* New York: Open Court.

Acknowledgements

I would like to thank Hannah Kittle, Rope Kojonen, Benjamin Elmore, Dustin Crummett, and David Worsley, for valuable comments and discussion on the manuscript for this work.

For Rosie

Cambridge Elements ≡

The Problems of God

Series Editor

Michael L. Peterson

Asbury Theological Seminary

Michael L. Peterson is Professor of Philosophy at Asbury Theological Seminary.
He is the author of *God and Evil* (Routledge); *Monotheism, Suffering, and Evil*
(Cambridge University Press); *With All Your Mind* (University of Notre Dame Press);
C. S. Lewis and the Christian Worldview (Oxford University Press); *Evil and the Christian God*
(Baker Book House); and *Philosophy of Education: Issues and Options* (Intervarsity Press).
He is co-author of *Reason and Religious Belief* (Oxford University Press); *Science, Evolution,
and Religion: A Debate about Atheism and Theism* (Oxford University Press); and
Biology, Religion, and Philosophy (Cambridge University Press). He is editor of *The Problem
of Evil: Selected Readings* (University of Notre Dame Press). He is co-editor of *Philosophy of
Religion: Selected Readings* (Oxford University Press) and *Contemporary Debates in
Philosophy of Religion* (Wiley-Blackwell). He served as General Editor of the Blackwell
monograph series Exploring Philosophy of Religion and is founding Managing Editor of the
journal *Faith and Philosophy*.

About the Series

This series explores problems related to God, such as the human quest for God
or gods, contemplation of God, and critique and rejection of God. Concise,
authoritative volumes in this series will reflect the methods of a variety of disciplines,
including philosophy of religion, theology, religious studies, and sociology.

Cambridge Elements ⁼

The Problems of God

Elements in the Series

God and Astrobiology
Richard Playford, Stephen Bullivant and Janet Siefert

God, Religious Extremism and Violence
Matthew Rowley

C.S. Lewis and the Problem of God
David Werther

God and Happiness
Matthew Shea

God and the Problem of Epistemic Defeaters
Joshua Thurow

The Problem of God in Jewish Thought
Jerome Gellman With Joseph (Yossi) Turner

The Trinity
Scott M. Williams

The Problem of Divine Personality
Andrew M. Bailey and Bradley Rettler

Religious Trauma
Michelle Panchuk

Embodiment, Dependence, and God
Kevin Timpe

The Problem of God in Thomas Reid
James Foster

God and Non-Human Animals
Simon Kittle

A full series listing is available at: www.cambridge.org/EPOG

For EU product safety concerns, contact us at Calle de José Abascal, 56–1°,
28003 Madrid, Spain or eugpsr@cambridge.org.

www.ingramcontent.com/pod-product-compliance
Ingram Content Group UK Ltd.
Pitfield, Milton Keynes, MK11 3LW, UK
UKHW021122170325
456354UK00009B/714